# He's
# SAVED...
# But Is He
# FOR
# REAL?

# He's SAVED . . .
# But Is He
# FOR
# REAL?

## KIMBERLEY BROOKS

HE'S SAVED...BUT IS HE FOR REAL?

A New Spirit Novel

ISBN-13: 978-0-373-83123-4
ISBN-10:    0-373-83123-4

www.kimanipress.com

**Printed in U.S.A.**

This book is dedicated to all the Sandy's, Michelle's, and Liz's of the world: He's saved, but does he fear the Lord, and does he have a real relationship with Jesus Christ?

## Acknowledgments

I would like to thank God for allowing me to live my dream of writing books—a dream held in my heart ever since I was a little girl. Thank you, Lord, for being my Best Friend, my Comforter, my Everything!

Thank you Mom, Lutricia Brooks, for having faith in my writing, and Dad, Lawrence L. Brooks, for compelling me to reach for the sky. A thank you shout out also goes to my stepmom Wallein Brooks. Thank you big sis, Kelley, for being my biggest cheerleader! Thank you to my entire family for being so supportive, ever since my first recital at elementary school.

Thank you to my closest friends for being there with listening ears, joyful moments or words of wisdom in due season.

I would like to thank my pastor, Bishop Keith A. Butler of Word of Faith International Christian Center, for teaching me the unadulterated Word of God, and for birthing in me a desire to know my purpose in Christ. Thank you, Bishop, and the entire first family, for not only talking the talk, but walking the walk. Thank you also, Evangelist Marie Diggs and Minister Catherine Eagan.

I would like to thank my editor, Glenda Howard, for seeing the potential in my work. Thank you to my agent, Karen Solem, for feeding my ego by reminding me how dynamic I am!

Thank you to the following Christian fiction authors I've had the privilege of meeting and being inspired by along the way: Jacquelin Thomas, Stacy Hawkins Adams, Kendra Norman-Bellamy, Brittney Holmes, Tia McCollors, Mata Elliot, Tiffany L. Warren, Venus Mason Theus, Sherri Lewis, Maurice Gray, Marilynn Griffith and Pat G'Orge-Walker. Thank you for proving numerous times that it *is* possible to write an entertaining and engaging story that still keeps Christ's principles at its forefront.

Also, to the many radio stations, print media, online magazines, television media, bookstores, churches, libraries, organizations, reviewers and book clubs: Thank you for your continued support!

To the best publicist in the business, Pam Perry of www.MinistryMarketingSolutions.com, thank you for encouraging me to be all that God has called me to be. I thank God for bringing you into my life as an awesome mentor and friend.

Last, but definitely not least, for everyone who read my first novel, *He's Fine...But Is He Saved?* and ran up to me and said, "Girl, I felt like I was reading my diary!" or "I'm not even a reader and I loved your book!" or "Sandy reminds me so much of myself" or "When is your next book coming out?": I pray that you enjoy this sequel just the same if not more. Thank you so much for your support. May God continue to bless you, and may you forever remain steadfast in Him.

# Chapter 1

*Oh, No, He Didn't!*

"Are you for *real?*" I asked Sandy while on my cell as I lay sprawled out on my brown couch in my one-bedroom apartment in downtown Detroit.

"Yes, girl," Sandy replied while lying upright in her white canopy bed with pink sheets, adjacent to her grandmother Madear's bedroom.

"You mean to tell me Pierre called off the wedding?" I asked.

I could not believe it. I couldn't believe that the first saved man I dated for eight months, fell in love with, then was dumped by so he could be with the wonderful "Miss Erika" called off the wedding. Erika Richmond, Minister Richmond's daughter, was supposedly the most virtuous prize in the church.

"Uh-huh," Sandy said as a matter of fact.

"Who told you?"

I had to ask. Knowing Sandy, this could be just some rumor. Or maybe a nightmare I needed to be awakened from.

"Madear's hairdresser's cousin's best friend, Lajanee-qua, told me," Sandy assured me.

I held the phone in utter shock as I thought about how I'd fallen in love with this man and couldn't understand why he left me that day almost two years ago seemingly out of the blue, until I found out that he had already started going out with Erika around the same time he was going out with me. I thought he broke up with me because I refused to give in to him but then later found out that it was because he'd already had his sights set elsewhere.

Man. I was looking forward to the day I finally got Pierre's two-timing, wanting-to-have-his-cake-and-eat-it-too self out of my thoughts and life forever. I was looking forward to the day he pledged his "till death do us part" to Erika and I even thought about attending the wedding. Erika, whom I used to serve with in the youth department at our church some years ago, did send me an invitation in the mail. I was looking forward to their wedding as the final closure that I needed to finally get my mind totally off Mr. Pierre Dupree. Oh, well, I guess that won't be happening anytime soon.

"Mickey? Are you there?" Sandy asked after a long pause.

"I'm here, girl," I replied sheepishly.

"I know it's a lot to swallow," Sandy continued. "The nerve of him! First he claims he's so *in love* with you, then he dumps you for Erika, then he comes back and proposes to you and you turn him down, then he goes back to Erika to marry her—and now he calls off the wedding? Who does he think he is? I think he's a little confused, don't you?"

Now did she have to go ahead and remind me of what a loser Pierre turned out to be?

"I don't know, girl," I replied, not knowing what else to say while half listening, half in a daze. *Why didn't he just go ahead and get married?*

Once a man is married, then that's it for me. No casual flirting, no hugs—except maybe a really light church hug and tap while the wifey is present, but nothing more. I was ready to write Pierre off as out of my life forever. And now I find out he's not even going to go through with it?

"Well, don't worry about it, girl. He's gonna get his," Sandy reassured me. "Like Madear always says, what goes around comes around. You reap what you sow, right? He can't keep going around here breaking girls' hearts without thinking it won't come right back on him and bite his butt."

"You're right, girl. You're right." I can't believe I'm actually receiving advice from Sandra A. Moore, my high school classmate who, when I led her to the altar last year to get saved, could barely quote John 3:16.

I am definitely proud of Sandy's progress in her spiritual walk with Christ. I'm especially proud of how she has been able to move on since she was sexually assaulted and almost raped last year by Carter Maxwell, a high-profile Detroit attorney who Sandy had thought was the one. Thank God my boyfriend, David, busted in on him and almost beat the living daylights out of him just before Carter could have his way.

*Bzzzzzzzz.*

The apartment buzzer rang.

"Hey, Sandy, that's David. I gotta go."

"Okay, girl. 'Bye." Sandy hung up.

"Who is it?" I sang in the intercom, as if I didn't know it was David, who had agreed to come over so we could enjoy this lovely Saturday afternoon in June together.

"It's the man of your dreams," David bellowed in a voice deeper than normal.

I cracked up as I buzzed David inside the complex. Instead of immediately opening the apartment door so he could walk right in, I rushed to the bathroom to do a quick once-over in the mirror.

"Too bad my hair appointment isn't till Monday," I muttered as I combed my fingers through my hair, which was getting a little thicker at the roots. I placed a small safety pin inside the V neckline of my royal-blue sundress to make sure I wouldn't be offering any free peep shows. Besides, I don't want to be a stumbling block to my man of God. We're not married *yet.* I gotta admit, though, I am looking pretty gorgeous today. My makeup is tight, my outfit is right and I am ready to have some fun.

"Who is it?" I chimed again in a high-pitched voice as David knocked on the apartment door.

"Girl, if you don't open this door!" he yelled, pretending to sound frustrated.

I opened the door to the sweetest sight a woman would

ever want to see. There stood my man of God, short and slim with a brown baby face, looking extra cute with his light blue polo shirt and tan khaki shorts. And to think, before I agreed to go out with him, I used to think David wasn't my type because he wasn't exactly six-foot-four. The more I've gone out with him and gotten to know him over these past fourteen months, the more I realize he's a saved woman's dream come true.

Playing along with his antics, I stood in the doorway and accusingly placed my hand on my hip. "Now, I know you not gettin' all huffy with me, Mr. David Parker?" I asked with an attitude and a neck roll.

Staring at me with a huge smile, proving he was pleased by the sight which stood in front of him, David snatched me close and said, "Girl, come over here and give me a hug."

Rocking me from side to side, I tasted a bit of heaven as I got a whiff of his expensive cologne, which I'd bought him for his twenty-seventh birthday last month. I couldn't believe that it's already been a little over a year since that night at the hospital, as the two of us had been seated in the waiting room waiting to hear about Sandy's recovery from the incident with Carter. That was the night David openly professed his desire to be more than just church buddies.

Never in my wildest dreams did I think I would ever end up dating David Parker, the little guy with the big voice who sings lead on the praise team every other Sunday. Not only had I been convinced that he wasn't my type physically, I'd also thought of him for years as simply my brother in Christ. However, that night at the hospital David made it plain and clear that he was no longer interested in playing the big-brother role. He wanted something more, and I was more than happy to offer him that kind of relationship.

"Have a seat while I grab you a drink," I said, letting go of his grasp and heading toward the kitchen. "What would you like?" I asked while opening the fridge.

"Water would be just fine," David replied.

I should have known. David drinks more than eight glasses of water a day. He doesn't believe in drinking pop. He says it contains too much sugar and just rots out your teeth.

"One glass of cold water coming up just for you, my love," I stated and set the water and coaster on the glass coffee table and took a seat on the opposite end of the couch. David looked so cute in his new outfit that I had to make sure I sat far away so I won't be tempted to plant a wet one on his inviting lips.

We've been doing pretty good thus far. In the beginning of our relationship, David sat me down and explained to me how the most we would do in our relationship physically was hug and hold hands. He'd said it was mainly to protect himself because he knows how excited he can get sometimes if there is anything more. He hates the idea of starting something he can't finish.

When he initially said it, I must admit, that concept sounded foreign to me, as I wasn't on the level where I can honestly say I won't even kiss the man I'll one day marry. But since David initially laid out his expectations, we were still successfully abiding by them. I actually respect the fact that he is willing to take the proper precautions so as to avoid any compromising situations which may have the both of us crying and repenting at the altar the next day.

"So did you decide what we're going to do today?" I asked to break the silence of him just staring at me.

"I'm not sure," he said, still staring. "You look great, by the way."

"Thanks." I gave a shy smile with a sip of my water.

"Let's see..." he continued on with today's plans. "I'm not really feeling the movies today. What do you feel like doing?"

"I don't know. It is a nice day outside, so why don't we do something outdoors?"

"You're right. It is nice out. Hey, why don't we check out that go-kart racing place down the street?" David asked in his usual, overly excited tone. "I heard it's really nice. They have putt-putt golfing and everything!"

*No, he* didn't *just say go-kart racing?*

Not wanting to put a damper on his suggestion, I replied, "Um, that's a good idea...but let's pick somewhere else."

David didn't understand. "Why not? I like putt-putt golfing and you like the go-karts. I think it'll be perfect. It'll be a lot of fun."

*He just doesn't get it, does he?*

Not convinced, I replied, "I know, but let's just pick somewhere else. What about bowling or something?"

"Bowling? I thought you wanted to do something outdoors? Besides, you don't even like bowling. You told me the last time you went bowling all you bowled was gutter balls. What's wrong with go-kart racing? What, are you

scared I'm gonna run you over on the racetrack or something?" David asked with a chuckle.

"Look, let's just drop it, okay?" I snapped.

"Whoa, I didn't mean to—"

"I said I don't want to go go-kart racing, and that's it!" I
yelled. I must have scared him, because he looked at me
like I was from a different planet.

After an uncomfortable pause, David muttered, "Why,
Pierre used to take you go-kart racing or something?"

I shot him an evil look. "Pierre—I mean, David—why did
you even have to go there?"

"What, you're the one getting all def—"

"Nobody said anything about Pierre, and there you go
bringing him up!"

"I didn't mean to—"

"How could you be so insensitive?" I whined with a
wrinkled face.

"Insensitive? You're the one getting all upset just because
I mention the word *go-kart*. Whether or not Pierre used to
take you there shouldn't have anything to do with me—
with us. You're with me now, baby. You shouldn't even be
worrying about him," he said and grabbed my hand.

"You're right." I softened up, scooted over closer and
placed my hand on David's thigh. "I'm sorry I got all loud.
I just got a lot on my mind, I guess."

*Why did Pierre have to go and call off the wedding?*

"That's okay." David cracked a smile and kissed my
sweaty palm. If only David knew what my mind and heart
were going through right now.

"I know the perfect place to go!" David proclaimed as if a lightbulb had gone off in his head.

"Where?" I asked.

"You'll see. Let's go."

# Chapter 2

*The Call*

"Matthew, I've been thinking about something lately," Liz stated as she and Matthew Sr. strolled hand in hand along the boardwalk of the Detroit River at Belle Isle downtown. Matthew's son, Matt Jr., was home with his grandmother, who'd so graciously volunteered to watch him all day while Matthew and Liz enjoyed a Saturday afternoon together.

Matthew slowed down the pace. "What is it, sweetheart?"

Liz stopped, allowing the hem of her long navy-blue jumper dress and her free-flowing curly braids to blow in the brisk wind, sighed and finally said, "I'm thinking about retiring from teaching and pursuing full-time ministry."

"Oh," Matthew said and stopped in front of her, a little concerned. "Is that how you feel the Lord is leading you?"

Matthew knew how much Liz absolutely loved teaching

the second-graders at Bakersville Christian Academy. He was almost saddened knowing his son won't be her student anymore, seeing as how little Matt was going into the third grade in the fall. However, Matthew knew that was the best thing to do anyway since the school system probably wouldn't allow a teacher to teach a student whose father just happened to be her boyfriend.

"Yes," Liz admitted.

"Well, then, that's wonderful, Liz! Congratulations!" Matthew beamed and gave Liz a big hug, allowing her to feel the softness of his gray silk shirt.

Liz released herself from Matthew's warm embrace, then forced a smile as they continued to walk. "I got a little money saved up to tide me over for a few months. Mom's already agreed to come down on the monthly rent that I pay her while staying at home, and I've already started receiving speaking invitations just from speaking at the women's center once a month. God's going to have to take care of the rest."

"And that He will," Matthew assured her and held her hand.

"Oh, and last week I registered my ministry as a nonprofit organization. It's called Zoe Ministries."

"Zoe Ministries," Matthew repeated. Being the Bible scholar and volunteer minister at his church that he was, Matthew knew that Zoe was the Greek word for "life," which describes the God kind of life—or life as God would have it.

"Got a nice ring to it," Matthew concurred.

Just then a tall, slender, honey-complexioned woman

with long brown hair jogged by in a black sports bra and short white shorts. Liz sneaked over to see if she could catch Matthew eyeing her.

"What?" Matthew asked innocently.

"Did you look at her?" Liz asked in all seriousness.

"What do you mean, did I look at her?"

"The woman that just went by—did you look at her?"

"Well, I couldn't help but *see* her. I have eyes, you know, so I know she was there."

Liz gave Matthew an accusing glare. "I know you *saw* her, but did you *look* at her?"

Matthew chuckled. "What? Now, I know you don't think I'm looking, in whatever way you want to call it, at some other woman? Liz, you know I only have eyes for you," Matthew assured her and then stopped and addressed her face-to-face as he wrapped his arms around her full-figured frame. "You're the only one I'm interested in, Elizabeth Marie Coleman," he added with a peck on her cheek. "I got tunnel vision, baby."

"Uh-huh," Liz murmured, not really sure if she should believe him.

# Chapter 3

*Moving On*

Sandy hopped out of her canopy bed after talking to Michelle on the phone and decided it was about time she got dressed. Even though she hadn't really finalized any plans for the day, she hopped in the shower, then threw on her pink tank top and matching shorts and headed to the kitchen to grab a bite to eat.

Madear, Sandy's grandmother who'd raised her since she was six, normally cooked her a hearty breakfast during the week before she went to work as a management trainee at Braxton's department store, but on the weekends Sandy had to fend for herself. Besides, Saturday was Madear's bowling day. She recently joined a bowling league a few months ago, so now Madear had bowling on Saturdays and the bridge club with her girlfriends on Sundays. Lately it seemed as though Madear had more of a life than Sandy. But Sandy was on a mission to change that.

Sandy thought about calling Dustin. The two of them had finally exchanged numbers last Sunday after church. Sandy wondered why it had taken him over a year to get her phone number. When she originally met him at Sweet Georgia Brown's restaurant downtown last year, he'd acted as if she were the most beautiful thing on earth and he really wanted to get to know her better. However, that night Michelle and Liz had ended up ministering to him, and he'd ended up getting saved instead of getting Sandy's digits.

Michelle and Liz had invited him to their church, Hype for Jesus, and Dustin joined the church and then the choir months later. Sandy had already been a member of the choir and was shocked the day she spotted him in the choir stands. But when she approached him one day after rehearsal and told him how she was so glad that he decided to join the church and the choir, he'd acted as though he didn't know who she was. He'd just politely said he was glad he joined and that he was enjoying the teaching he was receiving every Sunday from Pastor Wilkins.

Sandy thought it odd that Dustin barely paid her any attention. When she'd first met him at the restaurant, he had put the moves on her so hard that he'd acted as though he would drink her bath water. Now he treated her like Sally Sue on the street.

Now, after over a year of seeing Dustin in the choir stands just smiling at her and not approaching her, Sandy had had enough. She was tired of being alone and she was ready to start dating. Michelle always said that the man you go out with should be saved, right? Dustin's saved now, so it's time for him to ask her out. He's had a year to grow in God, so he should be ready now, right?

So last Sunday after church, Sandy waltzed her petite self right up to Dustin, held small talk while rubbing her short black hair and purposely using her cream-colored hand to tap Dustin's shoulder every once in a while, found out he played the piano as well as sang, told him she may be interested in piano lessons one day and they eventually exchanged phone numbers.

It wasn't exactly a lie, Sandy concluded. Madear always told her she had long, slim, piano-playing fingers. And even though Sandy could never picture herself having enough patience to endure piano lessons, she figured it may be worth a try, especially with a Tyrese look-alike as her piano instructor.

In the kitchen, Sandy decided on a turkey sandwich with wheat bread for lunch, since it was lunchtime, even though she hadn't had breakfast, when her cell phone rang.

Sandy looked at the screen, which read "Private Caller." She immediately answered because she loved receiving private calls—they were such a mystery to her. It could be her mystery dream man on the other line. It could be Dustin calling from a mysterious location. Unfortunately for her, though, it was neither.

"Hey, baby girl, what's up?"

*Oh, no,* Sandy thought, *not Mark.* It was her ex-boyfriend from over a year ago. He was also the first man she'd ever slept with—and the last man she'd ever had sex with since she got saved and made a promise to God to never break His commandment again by having sex outside of marriage.

Sandy wondered why Mark was calling again, especially since she hadn't heard from him since she'd spotted him last year at the Kirk Franklin concert holding hands with some Kimora Lee Simmons look-alike. Sandy had been so hot that night after she saw him. Mark's cheap self, during the year that they were an item, had never taken her to any concert. The most they did was stay at home, watch TV and have sex, and the only places they frequented were movie theaters or video stores.

"Mark, what do you want?" Sandy asked. She wasn't about to give Mark the satisfaction of thinking she could possibly be happy to hear from him. No, she was ready to stand her ground.

"Now what kind of way is that to talk to the love of your life?" Mark asked.

"You are not the love of my life," Sandy reminded him.

"How can you say that when we had so many good times together?" Mark whined in reference to their sexual escapades.

Sandy was onto him. "Call it what you want, but why are you calling me now?"

"I'm calling you because I love you, baby girl," Mark said, sounding more like a shady used-car dealer than someone who was sincerely in love.

"Mark, you don't love me! You love me like you love a pair of Jordans. You use me, then you throw me away!"

"Hold on now—if I don't recall, you were the one who broke up with me, sweetheart," Mark reminded her.

"That was *after* you kept playing, coming over here talking about how you were all saved and then trying to have sex with me again. Remember that? You played me for a fool! And what about Miss Thang I saw you with at the Kirk Franklin concert, huh? Did you forget about her?" Sandy was enjoying her ability to go off on Mark without giving in to his boyish pleas.

"Who, Tai? My ex? We got a divorce," Mark admitted.

"A divorce?" Sandy asked, stunned. "When did y'all get married?"

"Oh, we got married three months ago and got divorced last month."

"Last month? It's finalized already?"

"Yeah, we had it annulled, so it didn't take long. But enough about her—"

"Wait, wait, wait a minute, Mark." Sandy rubbed her temple as she took a seat at the kitchen table. "You mean to tell me you married that chick after only dating her for less than a year?"

"Yeah. I made a mistake, okay? I thought she was the one. I was wrong."

"Apparently," Sandy said. Even though she felt she was ready to be married, like, yesterday, Sandy was not about to marry anybody that quickly. She had made up in her mind that she had better sense than that. Besides, she'd never thought of Mark as the marrying kind. She guessed he figured since he thought he found his trophy bride, he wanted to hurry up and snatch her up before she eventually found out how he really was. Seems like the lucky choice found out a whole three months after the fact.

"So is that why you're calling me now—because you just got divorced?" Sandy asked.

"I'm calling you because I realize that I was wrong in choosing Tai. I should've chosen you. You've always been the only one for me, Sandy. I just couldn't see it then."

"But you know how I feel," Sandy said in reference to her celibacy pledge until marriage.

"I do. I'm cool with that. I can respect that. We don't have to have sex. I told you I was saved, too, right?" Sandy did remember Mark's sister Sheila, an Evangelist, telling her her little brother finally got saved after years of praying for him. Sandy still wasn't one hundred percent sure whether or not to believe he was totally sold out for God this time.

"Yeah, you say you're saved, but are you for real?" Sandy asked.

"What?"

"Are you for real? Do you really love God enough that you don't want to break His heart? Or are you just playing church?"

"I love God, Sandy. You know I do."

*Maybe he is sincere this time,* Sandy thought. *People deserve a second chance, right, Lord? I guess in Mark's case it would be a third chance. Or would it be fourth?*

"I don't know, Mark."

"C'mon now, baby girl, why don't you just let me come over so we can talk to each other in person. I'm serious this time."

"Why you always want to come over?" Sandy whined in frustration. "Why can't we ever go out?"

"Girl, you know how it is with the economy right now. It's hard out here for a brotha these days. Money is tight!"

"Oh, money is tight, huh? Is that what you told your ex-wife when you bought her her wedding ring—money is tight right now?"

"Sandy, what are you talking about?" Mark asked in a flustered tone. "You—you don't sound like yourself."

"You're right, Mark. I'm not myself. I found out that I had to die to myself so that I can live totally for Christ." Sandy liked the way that came out. She was happy she'd spent an extra half hour in prayer this morning. She felt extra powerful.

"Well, if that's the case, then I don't like this new Sandy. I want my old Sandra A. Moore back. I want my baby girl!"

"Well, you won't get her back!" Sandy stood her ground and meant it this time.

"What?"

"Oh, and one more thing, Mark—don't call me anymore." Sandy turned her cell upside down and yelled loudly in the speaker, "I'm through with you!"

Sandy clicked the phone off, happy to close that chapter in her life. Now time for her to open a new one.

She searched her purse for Dustin's number she'd scribbled on the back of a receipt.

# Chapter 4

*Breakfast Blues*

The inside of The Breakfast House was packed, as usual. A diverse crowd of suits and ties and blue jeans filled the seats of the intimate restaurant with the gold and red decor. Even though it was well into the afternoon, anytime, for me, is a good time for breakfast. They serve breakfast round the clock, and the service is superb.

A polite waitress led me and David to a table for two in the center of the floor. David pulled out my seat and I graciously sat down.

"How did you know I was in the mood for breakfast?" I asked.

"I told you—I know my woman," David said with a sly grin.

"Oh, really," I said, smiling in return.

Maybe he does know me more than I think he does.

Hopefully he can't read my thoughts. Even though I was sitting there with a saved woman's dream come true, my mind drifted again to thoughts of Pierre. Today Pierre should be enjoying his honeymoon on an island some- where, but instead he's somewhere out there—still single.

*Mmm, mmm, mmm.* I shook my head. I guess David won- dered what I was shaking my head about as I positioned myself more comfortably in my seat.

"What? What's wrong?" he asked, attentive as always to my every need and concern.

Even though I love the fact that David really cares for me and is very responsive to my needs, sometimes I think maybe I secretly don't like that about him, for fear that he would end up being a yes-man or something. I mean, if we got married, I wouldn't want his everlasting reply to be "Yes, dear" all the time. I want a man who can tell me no some- times. Call me crazy, but that's attractive to me. Pierre, on the other hand, would never be any woman's yes-man. He was much too smooth for that.

"Oh, nothing," I finally replied while grabbing the gold menu. As I read the selections, I thought I heard Pierre's voice in my head.

I kept hearing his voice, until I finally looked over at a corner on the right side of the restaurant. Sure enough, next to a floral display, there was Pierre, looking fine as wine in a cream linen pant suit, enjoying breakfast with a beautiful woman who looked like she could audition for the next season of *America's Next Top Model.*

I looked back down at the menu and looked up again

at the same corner. Pierre was still there—talking, smiling, laughing and having a good ole time.

Of all places, why did David have to pick the one place where I would run into my ex?

Well, I guess Pierre got over Erika pretty fast. Pierre always did have that bounce-back ability.

The waitress returned and took our orders. Since I really hadn't concentrated much on the menu, I just ordered my usual.

Upon the waitress's departure, I kept looking over at the corner where Pierre was dining with the beauty queen. After not seeing Pierre for almost a year—except for catching a glimpse of him during Sunday morning service because, once again, he had stopped going to early morning prayer—he still looked as good as ever. Even from fifty feet away, his chestnut skin was still as smooth as a baby's bottom, his hazel eyes were still mesmerizing and his smile could still put a sister under a spell.

David must have noticed my continuous shifting of the eyes, as he turned around in his chair to see what had my attention. When he spotted Pierre and his date, David snapped back around, threw his napkin on the table, frowned and said, "Excuse me, I have to go to the restroom."

I didn't think he should have gotten that upset. David can be such a baby at times. Instead of dealing with an issue head-on, he has a tendency to shy away from it by running away. I doubt if he truly had to go to any restroom.

I hadn't realized that Pierre even noticed I was in the

room, but as soon as David headed for the restroom, Pierre arose from his table and headed my way.

"Excuse me, is this seat taken?" Pierre asked me.

*How classic is that?* Besides, he knew it was taken. He knew my man had already warmed that seat.

"Actually, it is," I responded drily, not wanting him to know that my stomach was suddenly filled with butterflies and that my hands suddenly grew sweaty. I didn't know Pierre still had that effect on me. I guess the fact that he's no longer taken brought back those kinds of feelings inside.

I checked his ring finger to make sure he wasn't "reengaged" to this new woman seated at the table in the corner. There was no ring. I almost felt like accepting one of Sandy's mantras: An unmarried man is an available man, whether he's dating or not. Then again, I decided against that. I didn't want to disrespect my sister in the corner, who was reapplying her lipstick from a gold lipstick case at the table.

"Well, I think I'll have a seat anyway," Pierre responded and took a seat.

How rude. I just told this man the seat was taken, but he decides to sit down anyway? David could come back any minute now.

Then again, it was that same boldness that I loved about Pierre. He definitely was a man who got what he wanted, including my heart. Right now, though, I have to guard and protect it so he won't steal it again.

"So how are you, beautiful?" Pierre asked in a chipper tone.

"Pierre, David will be back any minute. And don't you have a date waiting for you?" I asked while motioning my big brown eyes to the corner table.

"Oh, Roxanne? That's my cousin from out of town. I just wanted to give her a taste of 'the D' by bringing her to one of the hottest breakfast spots downtown."

*His cousin?* I wasn't sure if I believed him. Then again, he did leave her table to come and harass me.

"Your cousin?" I asked.

"My cousin Roxanne, from Philly."

"Oh, I didn't know you had family in Philly."

"I do. I have family all over the place. Now enough about me," Pierre said and then grabbed my right hand from off the table. "How are you, Miss Lady?"

"I'm fine," I said sternly and snatched my hand back and placed it in my lap. "I'm also very happy in a fulfilling relationship right now."

"Fulfilling? Are you sure about that?" Pierre asked with a raised brow. I loved it when he raised his eyebrow like that. He looked sooooo sexy.

*Help me, Lord!*

"Yes," I assured him, even though I wasn't quite sure if my proclamation was just a faith confession or an actual fact.

"Well, I'm very happy for you," Pierre replied. "As for me, I don't know if you heard, but I called off my wedding to Erika."

"Oh, really?" I replied, not wanting to let on that Sandy had just told me he'd called off the wedding, so he wouldn't know that I was even thinking or talking about him once again.

"I did. I couldn't go through with it, especially when I realized I didn't love her...the way I loved you."

My eyes stared at my lap.

At that moment I wished I had a magic wand so—poof—he could just go away.

"Did you hear me, Michelle?" he asked while searching for my eyes. "I said I didn't love her the way I loved you."

"I heard you, Pierre," I managed to say. *Where is he going with this?*

Pierre grabbed my left hand this time, looked at me with glassy eyes and confessed, "I still care about you, Michelle."

"But, Pierre, I'm in a—"

Pierre used his free hand to shush my lips. "Shhh," he said. "Don't say another word, Michelle Williamson."

I couldn't do anything but just stare at him. It was like he had me in a trance. With that, he added, "I'm willing to fight for you, girl."

Reality suddenly smacked me in the face as I looked up and saw an angry David Parker standing at the table.

"Excuse me," David said to Pierre, suggesting Pierre rise up from his seat. I had never seen David look so angry. His eyes looked red and his forehead was wrinkled.

"Pardon me, sir," Pierre said as he slowly arose. "I was just saying hello to an old friend."

Upon exit, Pierre turned around, looked at me and said, "Don't forget what I told you," and headed back to his table in the corner.

"What was that all about?" David asked, apparently no longer holding his tongue.

"What was *what* all about?" I asked, acting oblivious to his concerns.

"I go away for five minutes and here he comes trying to get all extra friendly."

"He just came by to say hi," I said. I had no idea why I was defending Pierre.

The waitress brought our food, and during the meal David barely said two words to me. He looked agitated the whole time. Such a baby.

I grinned and waved at Pierre and his cousin as they exited the restaurant. Pierre looked at me with hungry eyes that I refused to match with my own but instead returned to eating my French toast. David remained silent.

During the car ride home, David still did not say a word to me as he headed north on the Lodge Freeway. Instead he cranked up the volume on the latest Fred Hammond CD.

I eventually grew tired of his ignoring me and decided to break the ice. I turned the radio down and asked, "David, what's wrong?"

"What do you mean, what's wrong? Nothing's wrong. Why'd you turn down the radio? I really liked that song."

"David, quit playing. I know something's wrong. You haven't said a word to me since breakfast."

"I don't know what you're talking about," he responded casually.

*So now we're playing dumb?* I decided to cut right to the chase.

"Are you mad that Pierre came to sit at our table while you were gone to the restroom?"

"No, I'm not mad because of that," David responded truthfully.

I couldn't take it anymore. "Then what is it, then?" I just had to know.

David looked over at me, paused slightly and said, "I'm mad because you're still in love with him."

"What?" I was shocked. "What are you talking about? Still in love with him? What gave you that idea?"

"I saw the way you looked at him when he was talking to you."

"What, you were spying on me or something?" I knew it didn't take him that long to use any public restroom.

"That's not the point. The point is I said I know you, Michelle, and I know you're still in love with him. You've never, ever looked at me the way you looked at Pierre today. I *wish* you would look at me the way you look at him," David said with a crackling voice.

"What do you mean? Looks mean nothing, David. I'm with you. I want to be with *you*. If I wanted to be with Pierre, then I would be with him. But I don't. I want to be with you, David."

I could tell David didn't buy it.

For the rest of the ride to my place he gave me the silent treatment again.

The worst part is, I wasn't sure if I even bought it myself.

If I had to choose between the two of them, I'm not exactly sure who it would be.

David pulled into a parking space in front of my apartment complex and placed his silver Sebring in Park. I guess that was the end of our afternoon together; he didn't exactly ask if I wanted to go anywhere else afterward. Besides, Pierre's presence sort of put a damper on our afternoon of couple bliss together. I guess I'll just go in my place and read a book.

Instead of getting out to open my car door, David turned his music back down and shifted his body toward me.

"Do you love me, Michelle?" he asked in all sincerity.

"What do you mean, David? Yes, I love you." I do love him with the love of the Lord.

"But do you *love* me?"

I wasn't quite understanding.

He continued, "I'm not talking about agape love, which is the love God deposits in our spirits once we get saved so we can have unconditional love for mankind. I'm talking about do you love me with that romantic love? Do I have your heart, Michelle?"

I paused for a moment. I had to think about that one. Even though David and I had been a couple for a little over a year now, I'd never concluded that I was really *in love* with him.

Sure, he was a perfect boyfriend, but for some reason, in the back of my mind, I always compared him to Pierre and wished that he could be more like him. I figured once Pierre got married off, then I wouldn't have to think about him anymore or make any comparisons because I would feel that Pierre's getting married would be God's way of taking Pierre off the market of my heart. But now that Pierre was single again—and apparently was still interested in me—I wasn't quite sure where David stood in my life.

Maybe David was just someone I chose to be with simply because he was interested in me first. Maybe I was never interested in him at all but just liked the fact that he was saved, decent-looking, served in the church, available and was interested—not to mention his great singing voice and the fact that he was a true worshipper.

The more I thought about it, the more unfair I felt I must have been to David. He is so sweet, but I really and truly didn't love him like I should love him by now.

I guess my pause was too long for David to bear.

"I thought so," he said, and with that he concluded, "Michelle, I think we should end this relationship."

"What?" I asked in shock. "You're breaking up with me?"

"I think it's the best thing to do at this point. Obviously your heart isn't with me." David added, while looking down, "Your heart is somewhere else."

Even though I felt I should be defending myself at that point, assuring David that my heart *is* with him and that I do love him with all of my heart, my lips were paralyzed. Words would not escape them.

David got out of the car, opened my car door, grabbed my hand and said, "You are a wonderful woman, Michelle. I hope we can still be friends."

I was stunned but didn't want to let on how I truly felt. We gave each other a final cordial hug and I headed to my apartment complex.

* * *

Inside my apartment, I plopped on the couch and folded my arms, refusing to shed a tear. I had no idea a Saturday afternoon with my man—a man I've been dating for over a year and thought would one day be my husband and the father of my children—would turn out to be the day that he decided he didn't want to see me again.

I couldn't hold it in any longer; I wiped a single tear from my eye. Suddenly tears flowed from my eyes, down my bronze cheeks like rivers, landing on my blue sundress now wrinkled and stained with teardrops. Eventually my eyes burned and my hands grew moist from trying to wipe the seemingly never-ending tears away.

And to think all this happened because Pierre decided to show up at the restaurant the same time I was out with David. Maybe this was God's way of showing me that David's and my relationship lacked the backbone it needed in order to survive in the long run.

I can't blame our breakup on Pierre. Because even though Pierre physically manifested himself at the restaurant today with his cousin, a part of me realized that the moment I found out he called off the wedding to Erika he emotionally manifested himself, once again, inside my heart.

"Dear God, I need You!" I cried out loud. I needed to trust God at that very moment. I needed to trust that God has my best interest at heart and that He determines my destiny.

I kicked off my heeled sandals and curled myself into a little ball on the couch and closed my eyes. I forced myself to stop crying, then attempted to shut off all the noise going on in my mind and tried to focus on total peace. I had almost fallen asleep when my cell phone rang.

I reached for my purse off the glass coffee table, dug and retrieved my phone and looked to see who it was before answering it.

The caller ID read "Pierre Dupree."

# Chapter 5

*Three's Still a Crowd*

"Hello, may I speak to Dustin?" Sandy asked in the sexiest Marilyn Monroe–sounding voice she could muster. She knew it was he who'd answered the phone—who else could it be answering his cell?

"This is he," Dustin responded in his usual deep tone.

Sandy liked hearing the soothing sound of his sultry voice once again. It reminded her of the same voice that had tried to holla at her at the restaurant. Even though it'd been over a year since that night, Sandy knew that he still was interested in her. No man can get over her that fast.

Sandy stared at the ceiling as she lay on her back on Madear's gold-embroidered plastic-covered couch. "Hi, Dustin. This is Sandra A. Moore. Remember me? From the choir?"

"Oh, hi, Sandy. Yes, I remember you. How are you?"

"I'm doing real good. Hey, remember you said that you loved playing the piano?"

"Yeah?"

"Well, I've always dreamed of learning how to play the piano. Especially since I write songs in my spare time. And I was wondering if you could show me some basic keys—or, I mean, basic chords or something—to get me on the right track."

"Uh, sure. I guess I can help you out."

Sandy sat upright. "Great! Can I come over tonight?"

"Tonight?"

"Yeah, tonight." *What's so bad about tonight?* Sandy thought. "You do have a piano at your place, right?"

"Uh, yeah. I do. I guess you can come over. We can only practice for about an hour, though, because I do have other plans."

"Oh, well, an hour is fine. It should be just enough time to get me warmed up to the keys. Say about seven?"

"Seven is fine."

Sandy jotted down the address to his condo and hung up the phone. She pondered about what she was going to wear. Something sexy yet subtle. Something sweet but sassy. She had the perfect outfit in mind.

Sandy lightly tapped on the large wooden front door of Dustin's condo. Dustin peeped out the peephole, opened the door and motioned for her to come inside and have a seat as he disappeared to the back room, not even giving her a second look.

Sandy pouted as she took a seat on his burgundy leather couch and crossed her flawless bare legs. She wondered why he hadn't opened the door and stared at her in amazement, at God's beautiful creation which stood before him. Sandy wore a loose-fitting short, pink baby-doll dress and silver stilettos. Her short hair was in a spiky flip style, and she'd even taken the time to apply extra makeup and fake eyelashes, which she thought made her look extra glam. To her, she looked even better than when he'd tried to holla at her at the restaurant, but his response when he'd opened his front door made her feel as though she were dressed in a frumpy old T-shirt and jogging pants.

Folding her arms as she awaited Dustin's return, Sandy observed her surroundings. She had to admit, his place was definitely laid out nicely. The colors were vibrant and the style was contemporary. She noticed the burgundy leather love seat that was adjacent to the four-seater couch and a burgundy chair, which was positioned in front of the large silver flat-screen TV. A gold-and-glass coffee table was in front of her, and a burgundy, cream and forest-green large circular rug was underneath the table. African-style paint-ings and figurines surrounded the place, along with au-thentic greenery.

Sandy figured either Dustin's mom or he definitely had a flair for interior decorating. Everything matched so per-fectly. It was as if it had a royal yet contemporary look to it. It was the best-looking condo she had ever seen and looked like something straight out of a magazine.

Just then a tall, fine, light-skinned gentleman with green eyes and curly brown hair came to the front room with a glass of iced tea in his hand. He had on some fitted jeans, which hung just below his tiny waist, and a black-and-white-striped shirt with a big collar.

"How you doing?" he sang and placed his hand out to Sandy to greet her.

Sandy looked the man she had never seen before up and down. His nails were manicured better than hers, and she thought about how she needed to make a trip to the nail salon to get a fill-in on her own nails real soon.

"Hi," Sandy replied and offered her hand in return as the kind stranger gave her a light shake.

"I'm Donte'. Dustin's roommate and best friend."

"Oh, hi, Donte'," Sandy replied sheepishly. She hadn't known Dustin had a roommate.

"Dustin told me you were coming. He just had to go in the back to get something, but he'll be back up in a minute."

"Oh. Okay."

"Would you like something to drink, hon?" Donte' asked as he sashayed over to the large kitchen.

"I'll have some of what you're having," Sandy said with a smile.

"All righty. I'll get you some iced tea—less the cognac," Donte' added with a hearty laugh. Sandy gave a light laugh in return.

"Thanks," Sandy replied.

"Iced tea is the perfect drink for a hot day like today," Donte' responded as he handed Sandy her tea while fanning himself.

He took a seat, zeroed in on Sandy's feet and sang, "Ooh, girl, I just love those stilettos! You better work!" he added with a snap.

Sandy just gave a pleasant grin and took a sip of her drink while searching around the room.

"Hey, Sandy." Dustin entered the room looking as fine as ever in a white muscle shirt and black trousers. His muscles seemingly oozed out of his shirt as Sandy's light brown eyes grew wide.

Sandy arose as Dustin entered the room.

"Hi, Dustin," she said with a wide smile. She was ready to receive her compliments now, especially since she had spent a whole three hours getting ready. Instead she felt she was being eyeballed by the person she'd just met moments earlier, who sat in the love seat beside her. Donte' looked at her as though he had a major attitude, as if to say, *Who does she think she is?*

"Let's head over to the den, where the piano is," Dustin suggested. Dejected after not hearing a single compliment, Sandy headed to the den with Dustin.

A voice from the front room rang out, "Dustin, while you and your little friend from church have your piano lesson, I'm about to head out in a minute. I'll see you in an hour!"

*In an hour?* Sandy thought to herself as she heard the front door slam shut. *Was* he *Dustin's other plans for the night?*

# Chapter 6

*Not Perfect, Forgiven*

"I'm home, Mom!" Liz sang loudly as soon as she entered their two-bedroom home on Detroit's West Side. Liz didn't immediately see Ms. Coleman and the baby in the front room, so she figured they must be in the bedroom. Liz hoped she wasn't loud enough to wake her eight-month-old little brother, Joshua, who may have initially been sound asleep in his crib.

The old Pauletta Coleman would have cursed Liz out for entering the house making such noise, but ever since she'd recommitted her life to Christ eight months ago, just before the baby was born, Ms. Coleman had thrown her potty mouth out the door—right along with her cigarettes.

Liz opened her mother's bedroom door and saw Ms. Coleman seated at the foot of the bed, feeding baby

Joshua applesauce. Ms. Coleman, with a baby's Bible open on her lap, made funny faces at Joshua, who seemed so amused as he giggled with a face full of the sweet, healthy treat.

"Hey, Mom," Liz said in a normal tone this time and sat on the edge of the bed to greet baby Joshua.

"Hey, little man-man!" Liz said as she lightly rubbed baby Joshua's belly. Joshua smiled even brighter and giggled even more as he was now face-to-face with his big sister. Liz loved making Joshua smile, and calling him her "little man-man" always did the trick.

"Hey, little man-man!" Liz said again, this time with a squeeze of his bright, freckled chubby cheeks. Baby Joshua was definitely a spitting image of his light-skinned, freckle-faced father, Richard, who just happened to be the married man Ms. Coleman had had an affair with, who'd left her to go back to his wife just before he could discover that Ms. Coleman was pregnant with his baby.

Unfortunately Pauletta Coleman was all too familiar with the concept, as Liz's conception twenty-eight years ago also resulted in Ms. Coleman's fiancé-at-the-time's decision to leave her at the altar just before Liz was born. It was as if all of the significant men in Ms. Coleman's life left her, including her biological father, when she needed them most.

But there had always been one man in her life that had never walked out on her, and that had been her Lord and Savior, Jesus Christ. It had taken her only child, Liz, to show her how much God really loved her before Ms. Coleman finally realized that she needed Him in her life in order to survive. Now she had recommitted her life to God, attended church regularly and prayed and read the Bible to her baby, Joshua, every single day. She had made a vow between herself and God to live her life conducive to God's Word—or at least try. She realized that she wasn't perfect, by any means, but that she sure was forgiven.

"Hey, baby, what you doing home already on a Saturday afternoon? I thought you were going out with Matthew?"

"We did. We walked in the park. I told him about my decision to pursue full-time ministry."

"You did?" Ms. Coleman beamed. "What did he say?"

"He was happy for me. He congratulated me and basically said he would support me along the way."

"That's wonderful. That Matthew sure is a nice man. God smiled on you when he gave you that one, Elizabeth Coleman. He's such a blessing and he's so good to his son—and a minister on top of all that!"

"I know," Liz said drily. *And a man with a wandering eye,* Liz thought, but refused to tell her mom so she wouldn't ruin her angelic image of him.

"How is little Matt Jr., anyway?" Ms. Coleman asked in reference to Matthew's eight-year-old son, who was now motherless since his mother passed away two years ago because of breast cancer.

"He's doing fine. Nana watched him while Matthew and I went out today."

"That was nice of her," Ms. Coleman replied in reference to Matthew's mom. When Matt Jr. was first born, he couldn't pronounce the word *Grandma* or *Granny* so he somehow came up with the name Nana, and everyone has been calling her that ever since.

"If you ever need me to watch little Matt Jr., just let me know and he can hang out with us!" Ms. Coleman said as she rubbed noses with her first son.

Ms. Coleman had always wanted a son, but she'd never pictured in her wildest dreams that she would have one at the age of forty-five—and definitely not one as a result of an adulterous relationship. She'd been so close to having an abortion, until Liz had convinced her to not murder one of God's creations—a baby who shouldn't be punished for the mistakes adults make and who should be given an equal opportunity at life just like everybody else. Ms. Coleman was so glad she went through with it and gave birth to baby Joshua. Next to Jesus, he was the center of her joy.

"Thanks for the offer, Mom. I'll have to take you up on that one day," Liz replied as the phone rang.

Liz answered the phone on Ms. Coleman's nightstand. "Hello?"

"Where is that witch at?"

"Excuse me?" Liz didn't recognize the female voice on the other end.

"Where is she at? I want to speak to that tramp! Is my man over there?" proclaimed the angry voice on the other end.

"I'm sorry, ma'am, you must have the wrong—"

"No, I don't have the wrong number!" With that, the caller started swearing in the phone. "Either put her on the phone or I'm coming over there to get my man!"

"Hand me the phone, Liz," Ms. Coleman commanded and Liz obeyed.

"Hello," Ms. Coleman said as pleasantly as possible.

"Hello, witch! Is my husband over there? Apparently you didn't get it right the first time, you home wrecker! Tell Richard I said to bring his yellow butt home now!"

"Earnestine, I'm sorry, but Richard isn't over here," Ms. Coleman replied. Liz was amazed at Ms. Coleman's calmness. It was as if she was used to receiving these types of phone calls.

"Don't lie to me!" the caller yelled on the other end. "Put him on the phone!"

"Earnestine," Ms. Coleman continued, not wanting to raise her voice for the sake of the baby she held in her arms, "I am not lying to you. Like I told you before, I haven't talked to or seen Richard in over a year. He is not here. Please don't call my house again."

"Liar!" Earnestine screamed in the phone loud enough for Liz to hear. With that, Ms. Coleman hung up the phone.

"What was that all about?" Liz asked.

Liz remembered that an anonymous caller would call and hang up the phone when Ms. Coleman had been seeing Richard last year, but Liz couldn't remember actually talking to anyone, especially not anyone who screamed on the phone sounding like an angry black woman.

Ms. Coleman let out a huge sigh. "It looks like Earnestine Miller is going to be the cross that I have to bear."

"What do you mean? Who is Earnestine Miller?" Liz asked, even though she had a clue.

"That's Richard's wife. She's been calling over here lately, looking for him. I keep telling her he's not here, but she swears I'm lying to her." Ms. Coleman arose to place baby Joshua in his crib as his jubilance began to fade.

"Then why does she keep calling over here? You told her you hadn't seen the man in over a year," Liz said.

"I know. If you ask me, he's having another affair with somebody else. I just feel for whatever woman he's lying to this time," Ms. Coleman replied while tucking in baby Joshua.

"I feel for his wife, but she can't keep calling over here, talking all crazy and going off. We can't have that, not with the baby here and all." Liz pondered for a moment, then asked, "Does she even know about the baby?"

"Oh, no. I haven't even told her about Joshua. Not at all."

"Well, don't you think you should?" I asked. "It's not like he can be kept a secret forever."

"Why?" Ms. Coleman asked as if she'd never thought about telling her.

"I mean, as his wife, she has a right to know, don't you think? And what about child support? I'm sure she's going to notice the dip in Richard's paycheck and the electronic withdrawals from Friend of the Court."

"I'm not applying for child support. I don't want none of that man's money. Me and Joshua don't need his money," Ms. Coleman said, then sat back on the foot of the bed.

"But, Mom, child support isn't about accepting hand-outs, it's about making sure the child is supported financially by the father, who played a big role in his even being here."

"I know, but I don't need any child support. God is all the support I need. Besides, I didn't get any child support for you from your father, and you turned out just fine," Ms. Coleman assured her daughter.

"I know, Mom, but that's different. The child support is for the baby. It's not about you. The baby needs the money. I'm not going to be around here forever, and your job alone isn't enough to support you and baby Joshua."

"We'll be all right. I don't need any child support." Ms. Coleman's mind was made up as she got up and stared at her son falling asleep in his crib.

"But, Mom—"

"I said it and that's it," Ms. Coleman barked. Joshua's eyes perked up. Ms. Coleman said quietly, "Now drop it, okay?"

Liz arose from the foot of her mother's bed. "Fine, then. It's your decision." Liz stood beside her mother and tucked in baby Joshua, who was now going in and out of sleep. "But it's not the right one. Sometimes we gotta think outside of ourselves in order to get things done which are supposed to benefit other people."

"There you go again with your little self-righteous attitude." Ms. Coleman stepped away from the crib and added, with arms stretched out wide, "Let he who has not sinned cast the first stone."

"I'm just saying, Mom, it's not right. Have you even apologized to the woman?"

"Apologized? For what?" Ms. Coleman asked in defense.

"Apologized for causing disruption in her home. She and Richard have two teenagers, and your and his affair almost broke up their marriage. When she calls here going off on you, have you ever said, *I'm sorry?*"

Ms. Coleman folded her arms, rubbed her chin with her thumb and said, "No, I haven't."

"Why haven't you?"

"I haven't been led to, all right?"

Liz shook her head at that one. It never ceased to amaze her how some church folk feel they have to be "led" to do the right thing. Some stuff you don't need God to have an army of angelic hosts blow a trumpet at your front door about. Some stuff you just do because it's the right thing to do.

"Whatever, Mom. If you ask me, the sooner you apologize, the sooner you can stop that woman from calling around here like a crazy woman, asking for her husband. Then maybe she won't have to be the cross you have to bear, as you call it."

"Hmm, she's more like a thorn in the flesh." Ms. Coleman added dramatically, "A messenger of Satan sent to buffet me!"

"Everything is not always the devil's fault, Mom," Liz reminded her.

"Girl, go on get out of my room," Ms. Coleman said with a laugh and threw a pillow at her daughter and missed. "I'm tired of you!"

# Chapter 7

*Confused?*

I wasn't quite sure if I should answer my cell. I didn't want Pierre to know that I had been crying or that I was upset. However, by the third ring I accepted the call.

"Hello," I answered while clearing my throat, trying to sound as normal as possible.

"Hello, beautiful," Pierre replied in a sultry tone.

"Hi, Pierre," I said drily. His compliment didn't quite put a smile on my face as it usually does. However, hearing his voice again sure made a sister feel good on the inside.

"Hey, what are you doing tonight?" Pierre asked.

"I don't know. I'm probably staying in." I didn't want to admit to Pierre that I'd planned on staying in, watching a tear-jerker movie and munching on a box of chocolates to help alleviate my sorrow while keeping a box of Kleenex nearby so I can wipe the tears away.

"On a gorgeous night like tonight? We *must* go out!"

"We?" I asked. This man keeps forgetting that I have a boyfriend. Or shall I say *had* a boyfriend. *Now where's that doggone remote control?*

"Yes, we. Why, do you have other plans?"

Why was Pierre trying to act so oblivious to everything? It was as if he was trying to just pick up where we left off two years ago—before he dumped me.

"Why not? I, personally, think it's a great idea. I would love to see you again and I would be honored to be able to spend time with you and talk to you." After a slight pause Pierre added sweetly, "Please?"

"I don't know," I responded.

"C'mon, please, Michelle. I need to talk to you tonight. I'm serious."

I could tell he was serious this time. I just wasn't sure if I was ready for all this. Then again, why am I speculating? He may just want to get something off his chest. I'm sure meeting with him tonight will be painless. Besides, I don't have anything better to do tonight. And going out with Pierre would be better on my thighs then pigging out on a box of chocolates.

"Okay, I guess. We can talk tonight."

"Great. I'll pick you up at eight?"

"Eight is fine."

I must admit, it felt kinda weird walking arm in arm with Pierre along the shore of the Detroit River Walk at Hart

Plaza downtown. It felt weird, but I was somewhat relaxed. Listening to him go on about his life sort of felt like we were just two old friends getting reacquainted with one another. He still knew how to make me laugh and blush. He knew how to make me feel special just by being in his presence.

We stopped at the Gateway to Freedom bronze statue of a small group of adults and children looking ahead toward Canada, which was, at the time, a pit stop to freedom and liberation from slavery since Canada abolished slavery in 1834. The statue was an international memorial to the Underground Railroad.

"Isn't it amazing how Harriet Tubman was able to lead hundreds of slaves out of the South to safety?" Pierre asked as we admired the monument sculpted by Ed Dwight.

"Did you know that Detroit was one of the largest terminals of the Underground Railroad?" Pierre asked and I shook my head, with my shoulder-length hair blowing in the wind of the brisk summer evening. "Detroit's Underground Railroad code name was Midnight. At first, Michigan was the place where slaves escaped to freedom, then Canada became a safer place once slavery was abolished there in 1834. But once the Fugitive Slave Act passed in 1850, a lot of folks left Detroit and went on to Canada so they could remain free. Some did return after Emancipation in 1863, though."

It never ceased to amaze me how Pierre is such a black history buff. His appreciation for history and the arts was another quality about him that I truly admired. As he stood in awe, gazing at the monument, it made me start to like him all over again.

"Yes, amazing indeed," I replied as I put my hand inside Pierre's arm as we admired the monument together.

Pierre continued, "It's amazing to know and witness how far we have come as a race of people."

"That is true," I said while deeply gazing at Pierre more so than the monument. He turned to face me.

He must have noticed me shivering, as he took off his black blazer and placed it over my bare shoulders. I looked up at him and smiled as if to say, *Thank you.*

"You are so gorgeous, Michelle," Pierre said. "I am so glad to be looking into your big brown eyes once again."

I smiled.

"Why did you tell me, no?" he asked seemingly out of the blue. "Why couldn't you just give me a chance?"

I didn't know how to respond. Just looking at him made my heart beat fast. *God, he's so fine.*

I'd always wanted him, but I wanted him to choose me first. And now we were standing here together once again, lost in each other's eyes.

Suddenly my purse starting ringing. I opened my purse and pulled out my cell and saw that it was David calling me.

Pierre looked down at my phone and saw who was calling, as well, and softly whispered in my ear, "Don't answer the phone."

"Who do you think you are telling me not to answer my own phone?" I said with a slight laugh.

Pierre kept a serious tone and said, "He had his chance."

"But—"

"Shh." Pierre placed his finger on my lips once again like

he did earlier today at the restaurant. His shushing me placed me, once again, in a trance that I felt I could not escape. His large hands drew my face closer to his, then he kissed my lips ever so lightly and sweetly.

My phone kept ringing and ringing, until I eventually put it back in my purse. Soon the ringtone became the background music to my and Pierre's heartfelt kiss, until it finally went to voice mail.

My heart raced as Pierre rubbed his fingers through my hair as our tongues danced with one another. It felt so good kissing him once again, until I heard a small, still voice in my spirit say, *Slow down, Michelle.*

I slowly but surely drew back from his grasp and confessed, "Pierre—I can't."

Pierre looked at me, confused. But instead of responding with words, he grabbed me and held me in his arms, rubbed my back and let out a peaceful sigh.

I stood paralyzed in his arms as we held each other seemingly for hours and hours into the night until the stars began to spy on us.

Even though I wasn't quite sure what this night of reconnecting truly meant for our relationship—whether it marked a rekindling of an old flame or just a night of two heartbroken souls seeking comfort from one another—I must admit that it sure felt good to be back in Pierre's arms once again. Just like old times.

# Chapter 8

*It Can't Be Me*

Sandy made herself comfortable on the piano bench of the white baby grand as Dustin pulled out an old, worn music book. It looked so used and torn up Sandy figured it must have been his first piano book his mama taught him from when he was ten years old. He placed the book in front of Sandy on the piano and began the lesson.

"Here is middle C," Dustin pointed out while playing the note. "Now you play," he instructed.

Sandy felt as though he were the piano teacher and that she was his six-year-old student. She obeyed and played the note.

"Okay, here is how you position your hands on the keys." Dustin spread his fingers over the keys with his left and right thumbs positioned on the middle C on either side.

Sandy liked this part of the lesson. It's where she got to interact with his big, strong hands.

"Like this?" Sandy asked as she covered his huge hands with her own petite ones.

"Yes," Dustin said. "Like that," he added while looking at her with a sly grin.

"I like this part," Sandy added with a smirk.

Suddenly Dustin removed his own hands from the piano and proclaimed, "Okay, now to get back to this book." Dustin nervously fumbled through the pages. "This is a piece you probably can play."

A little disappointed by Dustin's response—or lack of a response—to Sandy's flirtatious attempt, she decided she'd try something else.

"Why don't *you* play that piece for me?" Sandy asked. "And I'll watch." With that, she arose from her seat and motioned him to sit down.

"Okay, sure," Dustin said as he proceeded to play the simple piece.

While he played, Sandy leaned over on the white baby grand piano while purposely sticking out all of her assets, hoping Dustin would try and sneak a peek. She placed her hand underneath her chin and smiled at Dustin as his fingers worked their magic on the black-and-white keys.

To Sandy's dismay, Dustin's eyes stayed glued to the music book. Not once did he glance over at Sandy. Not once did he make a single attempt to check her out. It was as if she were invisible and he was in his own world with his music, playing at a recital for a crowd whose only interest was to hear each note played perfectly as dictated by the old, raggedy music book.

After a while, Dustin closed his eyes. He was lost in the music. He was in a zone.

Frustrated, Sandy had had enough, stood up straight and asked, "Where's your bathroom?" as if to purposely snap Dustin out of his own little world.

Startled, Dustin replied, "Huh? Oh, it's down the hall, to the right."

Sandy made her way to the restroom, and Dustin closed his eyes once again.

Sandy stared at herself in the bathroom mirror. Funny, not a single strand of hair was out of place, and her makeup was still on perfectly. She checked her eyes to make sure her fake lashes weren't sliding off, and they weren't. She smiled to make sure there was no lipstick on her teeth, and there wasn't. Finally she breathed into her hands to make sure her breath was still fresh from the mint she'd just eaten, and it was.

Sandy looked again at herself in the mirror. "Sandy, girl, tonight you got a lot of work to do if you want to get this man," she said out loud. Then she remembered how Dustin had initially gawked at her when he'd first met her in the restaurant last year.

She concluded that this man isn't the same man she met a year ago and that he may have gotten involved in a relationship other than the newly found one he had in Jesus. She figured either this man is gay or she must be losing her touch. And Sandy refused to believe the latter.

# Chapter 9

*In God's Presence*

*"Rejoice in the Lord always, and again I say, again I say, rejoice!"* the entire three-thousand-member congregation sang right along with the praise team Sunday morning.

Michelle placed her small Bible and notebook on a purple cushioned chair located on the right side of the church, just ten rows from the front. After she'd cried out to God earlier this morning, she'd decided to just toughen up, take a shower and get dressed so she could leave early enough in order to get a good seat.

Michelle wasn't about to stay in a somber mood and was prepared to revitalize her spirit during the worship service, and her singing along during praise and worship before the message always did the trick. By doing so, it allowed her to take her focus off herself and put it totally on God.

Praising God reminded her of the victory she already had in Christ and made whatever problems or concerns she had before service seem so miniuscule and unimportant.

Before finding a seat, she couldn't remember if it was David's week to serve as praise team leader. However, now, seated just a few hundred feet from the stage, Michelle witnessed up close David's normal, energetic self bounce across the long stage with a wireless mic in his hand as he led the entire congregation in praise in worship.

Michelle could tell he was really into it this morning, as his hands were uplifted and his eyes shifted to both sides of the congregation as he encouraged everyone to take their focus off their problems and praise the Lord. His small, energetic frame moved from one side of the stage, adorned with a large purple floral arrangement, to the other side of the stage, which was adorned with the same beautiful arrangement.

Michelle wondered if he'd spotted her. He probably had; but one would never know since he was totally consumed with praising God. David's voice sounded so heavenly, like a hundred angels singing at God's throne. That was one of the things Michelle would always miss about him.

*"Come on now, let's praise His Name, praise His Name to the end of the earth...."* the congregation sang right along with the praise team.

As David continued to lead the church in song in his new brown suit and matching shiny shoes his mom bought him for his birthday, Michelle noticed that he seemed extra hyper this morning. His smile was a lot brighter, and he bounced around from one side of the stage to the other with such ease. Like the name of their church, Hype for Jesus, today David definitely was Mr. Hyper himself.

Michelle wondered if it was because he'd just broken up with her last night. Maybe his breaking up with her was the freeing that he'd needed, and his outward joy was a sign that their breakup was somehow ordained by God. He definitely could go on without her. It was totally obvious.

Maybe a little *too* obvious, Michelle thought.

The congregation switched to worshipping God as the pianist played the prelude to "Here I Am to Worship," which was one of Michelle's favorite worship songs. Every time she heard that song, she immediately lifted up her hands and bowed her head in worship to her Heavenly Father. The world stopped when she heard that song, for it reminded her that whatever she was doing at that moment, in the midst of all the hustle and bustle of everyday life, now was the time to say, "Here I am, God. I am here to worship You."

Michelle closed her eyes and harmonized with the congregation. She pictured herself seated at God's throne and bowing down along with the angels and heavenly hosts.

Tears like rivers flowed from her eyes as she thought of God's goodness, His awesomeness and how faithful He had been and always would be to her. She took her mind off everything else and simply began to worship Him from the depths of her soul. Michelle barely noticed the blue-coated usher politely offering her a Kleenex until her neighbor tapped her and Michelle gladly accepted a few tissues.

Once the pianist played the final chord of the song, the congregation continued to worship the Lord. Everyone, in one accord, kept harmonizing and humming and singing in the Spirit, so much so that it actually sounded like a choir of angels.

Michelle squeezed herself tightly, dropped to her seat and keeled over in worship. One by one, church members flooded the wide purple-carpeted altar in order to worship God. Michelle eventually arose and went up to the front and kneeled down at the altar herself.

She sang in the Spirit as she worshipped God and thought about His goodness in spite of herself. She thought about His love, which is everlasting, and His mercy, which endures forever.

The entire congregation continued to worship God for another twenty minutes, until finally everyone began to filter back to their seats.

"Hallelujah," the young, slender, twenty-eight-year-old Pastor Wilkins proclaimed as he approached the pulpit in a conservative gray suit. "There is definitely a sweet Spirit in this place," he stated, and some church members replied with a hearty, "Amen!"

Michelle's ears perked up as she received confirmation about what she was struggling with internally regarding her feelings for Pierre and her desire for a mate.

It amazed her how, even with a congregation of three thousand members, every time she attended service she felt as if she were sitting on a couch, spilling out all of her problems to her pastor and then receiving, line by line and precept upon precept, what she was supposed to do about the situation.

She was so grateful that God loved her so much, that He would give her pastor a word that was seemingly tailor-made just for her.

Michelle ended up with pages and pages of notes from the sermon and planned on praying over and studying them even further when she got home.

After service, Michelle headed straight to the lobby to look for her friends, Liz and Sandy.

"Hey, Michelle!" Liz spotted Michelle from across the lobby and the two of them met each other halfway and gave each other a hug.

"I love your outfit. You look good, girl!" Liz said, complimenting Michelle's cream pant suit and gold stilettos with matching gold clutch purse.

"No, that's you, girl. Mr. Matthew Long betta watch out!" Michelle said in reference to Liz's long black dress with large silver flowers all over, hanging loosely yet comfortably.

Liz laughed out loud and covered her mouth.

"So how have you been, stranger?" Michelle asked Liz, making reference to the fact that she hadn't heard from her in over a week.

"What are you talking about?" Liz asked.

"Folks get a man, then act like they can't call anybody anymore," Michelle stated.

The two of them laughed. "Girl, you are so crazy," Liz continued. "And I know *you* not talking, Miss I'm-dating-the-praise-team-leader-so-I-don't-have-*time*-for-anybody-else-anymore. I think you're just telling on yourself and trying to put it on me!"

"I don't think so. And, anyway, I don't have to worry about *that* anymore."

"About *what* anymore?" Liz asked.

Michelle walked closer to Liz and whispered in her ear, "David broke up with me last night."

"What!" Liz yelled, causing a few heads in the church lobby to turn in their direction. Liz had forgotten where she was for a moment. "What do you mean? Girl, we gotta talk."

"Hey, y'all!" Sandy sang as she sashayed—her petite frame encased in a formfitting pastel-pink dress—right in the middle of Michelle and Liz's conversation. "What's going on?" Sandy asked, feeling left out. "What's all the whispering about? Michelle, I saw you whispering in Liz's ear. I want to be let in on the secret!"

"Girl, I'ma have to tell you later, *outside* the church house. No telling who else may be listening." Michelle looked around to make sure she didn't see David.

"Okay, well, why don't we do brunch?" Sandy suggested. "You know they have that gospel brunch at the Grand City Grille downtown on Sundays. How does that sound?"

Michelle and Liz looked at each other. Since Michelle didn't have any immediate plans for the rest of the day, she responded, "Hey, sounds good to me!"

"You down, Liz?" Sandy asked.

"I'm down. Let's all follow each other and meet there."

* * *

"Okay, so I get to Dustin's condo and he lets me in. Do you know this joker didn't even say one single thing about how *good* I looked?" Sandy stated as she munched on her Caesar salad.

"No!" Liz proclaimed sarcastically as she poured syrup on her waffle.

The three ladies had chosen a table in the center of the restaurant, which gave a perfect view of the stage where a Caucasian male serenaded the crowd with traditional gospel tunes.

"Girl, he had the audacity to not say a word, then he just disappeared to the back. Then, when he left, out comes his so-called male roommate, who had on an outfit that was sharper than mine! Girl, his shoes were so clean it looked like you could eat off 'em! And he acted so sweet he could close down a sugarcane factory!"

"Sweet, so you mean he was gay?" Michelle inquired while taking a bite of her herb-roasted double chicken breast.

"He was about as gay as I'm short. He claimed to be Dustin's best friend, but I could see past that foolishness. He was grilling me when Dustin finally came back in the room to tell me about our piano lesson."

"So how did that go?" Liz asked.

"Go? It didn't! Dustin barely paid any attention to me!" Sandy retorted.

Liz laughed lightly. "I meant how did the piano lesson go?"

"Oh, it went all right, I guess. I didn't learn anything," Sandy said with a disappointed look on her face.

"What? How can you not learn anything?" Michelle asked as she ate a forkful of macaroni and cheese.

"Shoot, I wasn't there for any piano lesson, I was there to teach *him* a little somethin' somethin'!" Sandy added with a snap.

Liz almost gagged on her water after hearing Sandy's admission.

"Oh, excuse me, Liz, I didn't mean that," Sandy said. "I forgot your holier-than-thou self can't take me making comments like that," she said and smiled sarcastically.

"Whatever." Liz rolled her eyes. "Besides, you're just saying he's gay because he didn't try to hit on you."

"That is not true!" Sandy defended herself. "Any man in his right mind would try to holla at me! Or shall I say any *straight* man. Watch this."

Just then a tall, handsome, brown-skinned man in a shiny black suit walked by their table.

"Excuse me," Sandy said to the stranger, who turned around immediately and came over to their table.

"Well, hello," the man said, staring intensely at Sandy.

"Hello, yourself. You know what, I'm sorry I interrupted you—I thought you were someone I know, but you aren't him."

"Well, I wish I was!" the man continued in a voice deeper than Billy Dee Williams's. "I may be someone you don't know right now, but I may be someone you should *get* to know."

Sandy gave him a flirtatious grin.

"Why don't you give me a call sometime," he said and

reached over to give Sandy his card while keeping his eyes on her.

Reaching over, he mistakenly knocked over a glass of water that spilled all over the table.

"Oh, I'm so sorry!" the man said, embarrassed, and scrambled to wipe up the spilled water with the nearest napkin.

A waiter immediately noticed the spill and came over to help.

"I'm so sorry about this," the man said. "I can be so clumsy at times, especially when I'm caught off guard by such a heavenly sight as you."

Sandy gave a shy smile. "That's okay. You didn't mean to do it."

The man said, "What was that, water? I'll tell you lovely ladies what—all drinks on me! Whatever you have, I'll cover the tab! Now how does that sound?" he propositioned as the waiter finished drying off the table. Fortunately none of the water spilled on anyone's clothes.

Sandy looked around at the rest of the ladies as Liz and Michelle just looked at each other.

"Sounds good to me!" Sandy said. The man successfully gave Sandy his card this time and said, "Give me a call sometime," and left the now-dried table along with the waiter.

"Maybe," Sandy replied with a smile and a wink and gazed at the card as the man walked away. "Hmm, Jerome Simmons, real-estate agent. Maybe he can hook a sister up with a house," Sandy said and was about to tuck the business card in her bra when Liz said, "Girl, give me that card!" then snatched the card right out of Sandy's hand.

"What? Don't hate. I told you I can get any man I want."

"Didn't you see that man's ring finger? That man is married!" Liz said.

"Oh," Sandy stated. "I normally look at the finger first, but I guess I didn't this time since I was trying to make a point."

"Well, you made your point. Next time try not to make it with a married man!" Liz exclaimed.

"Dang, Liz. I didn't know, okay? You act like I'm about to call him or something."

Liz didn't say a word.

"Well, I'm not! Gee. You gotta give me some kind of credit," Sandy said.

"You know," Michelle began while eating a forkful of food, "it never ceases to amaze me how some married men hand out their phone number like candy or flirt with single women, knowing good and well that when it's all said and done they're still going home to be with their wife."

"I read somewhere that married men have affairs as a form of escape from reality," Liz added. "Isn't that crazy?"

"It sure is. And selfish, if you ask me," Michelle piggy-backed off Liz. "And the sad thing is, both saved and unsaved men act the same way sometimes."

"I know!" chimed Sandy, folding her arms and frowning at the married escapist from the other table, who kept his eyes on her.

"Well, anyway…" Sandy attempted to focus the attention back on her original experiment. "Even though he's taken…I told y'all I can get any man I want! I had that man eating out of the palm of my hand! He better be glad he *is* married, otherwise he'd be buying us all dinner right about now. Men are so easy!" Sandy giggled like a little girl.

"Oh, waiter!" Sandy sang, flailing her hands in the air toward the waiter. "May we have another round of drinks, please? Sprite on the rocks!"

"Whatever," Liz replied and rolled her eyes again. "We can all catch a man if we throw ourselves at one like you just did." Michelle lightly kicked Liz underneath the table out of habit. Liz proceeded to smile at Michelle and wink her eye wildly at her as to imitate their not-shy-at-all friend.

Michelle couldn't control herself any longer. She burst out laughing, and Liz did, too. Eventually Sandy joined in on the laughter.

"Both of y'all need to just leave me alone!" Sandy said. "Y'all just hatin' on a sista 'cause I got it!"

"Yeah, you got it, all right," Liz said. "*What* is the question." Liz and Michelle laughed again.

Liz continued, "Anyway...back to you, Miss Michelle. Now what were you telling me after church? You mean to tell me you and David broke up?"

"What?" Sandy asked in shock. "When did all this happen?"

"Yesterday," Michelle confessed.

"What happened?" Sandy asked. She demanded an explanation. She'd been looking forward to one day buying her very first bridesmaid dress for David and Michelle's wedding, and now they weren't dating anymore? What was the world coming to?

"Well," Michelle began, "David seems to think I'm still in love with Pierre, so he broke up with me."

"In love with Pierre—is that true?" Sandy asked with brightened eyes.

Michelle just looked at Sandy and Liz with no reply, feeling guilty as ever.

"Whoa, whoa, whoa, wait a minute," Liz said. "You mean to tell me you are still in love with Pierre, after he dogged you out?"

"He didn't dog me out," Michelle pointed out. "I was the one who refused to marry him, remember? David dumped me yesterday after we ran into Pierre at the Breakfast House, then Pierre and I kinda went out last night and old feelings started coming back. And those feelings were so real this time."

"What, as if the other times they were fake?" Liz asked.

"Just forget it," Michelle stated. "You guys obviously aren't helping me out here."

"Wait a minute, now, Michelle, we *do* want to help. We're just trying to hear where you're coming from," Liz stated. "Because to me it sounds like you're giving up probably the best man that could ever happen to you for one that is selfish and only cares about playing with some woman's mind and heart so he can get what he wants and then leave."

"What makes you think he would leave?" Michelle asked sincerely.

"Well, he left Erika," Liz reminded her. "He bailed out of the wedding at the last minute, right?"

"I know, but he said he left her because he wanted to be with me." Michelle knew her comment sounded self-centered, but she wanted to somehow believe his motives were sincere.

Liz let out a huge sigh. She was trying to understand where her best friend was coming from and she didn't want to see Michelle get hurt again. "Michelle..." Liz continued.

Sandy remained as quiet as a church mouse as she sipped on her second Sprite, compliments of the married man with the shiny suit.

"What do you see in this man?" Liz asked. "Why do you like him so much? What kind of a hold does this man have on you?"

Michelle thought about it a moment, then began to spill her heart.

"I don't know. It's just something about him. Of course, he's fine. He loves God—or at least has a heart for Him and serves His people. And he's so...romantic. He always says the right things that send chills up and down my spine."

Sandy listened to Michelle with a smile and dreamy eyes, with her hand cupped underneath her chin.

Michelle continued, "He's saved, but he's so down-to-earth and so sexy to me. Is there something wrong with wanting to be with somebody who is saved and sexy? Is that, like, an oxymoron or something?"

Sandy shook her head no.

"To me, Pierre is, like, so real," Michelle continued. "He's aggressive and firm—he says what he wants, he gets what he wants and he's so outgoing and charming. He's real charismatic, and I like that about him. He's smart and ambitious and a genuine leader in the community. He wants to help other people with his Internet business and he even said he's thinking about starting a credit-repair business for local people with bad credit."

"Wow," Sandy replied.

Michelle continued, "His presence commands attention and his voice is so soothing. I can listen to him speak all night. And every time I'm with him he makes me feel like a queen." Michelle picked up a napkin and wiped the corner of her eye. "I just want to be with him. Is there something wrong with that?"

"But what about David?" Liz asked.

Michelle smiled as she thought about David. "David's a sweetheart. He is definitely a saved woman's dream come true. He loves the Lord, obviously, and he loves his mom to pieces. He's very well mannered and polite and he's very loyal and has been very faithful to me."

"In other words," Sandy interjected, "bo-ring!"

"Boring? I don't know about all that," Michelle said.

Sandy let Michelle continue. "He does have visions and dreams. He wants to be a gospel recording artist one day, traveling across the country. But I just don't see that happening for him. I mean, I can see it happen, because anything is possible with God, but I don't really see him doing anything right now to help make it happen."

"Well, maybe that's why God has you in his life—to help motivate him to follow his dreams," Liz added.

"I know. But him living with his mama in the basement and working in the meat department at a grocery store isn't really helping him work toward living his dreams."

"So you don't like him because he lives at home and doesn't have what you consider to be a good job, is that it?" Liz asked. "He couldn't help the fact that he got laid off from the plant. He had to get another job somewhere."

"No, that's not it at all," Michelle tried to convince herself. "It's just that he's not exciting. He's like a yes-man, and I don't want that in a man. I want somebody who's ambitious and fun. I want somebody who is willing to tell me no sometimes."

"Have you prayed about it?" Sandy asked Michelle the question that Michelle normally asks her.

"Yes, I have," Michelle responded with lowered eyes.

"Well?" Liz asked, trying to locate Michelle's eyes once again.

"I believe God wants me to be patient and wait on Him," Michelle confessed.

"Sounds like a Word from God to me," Liz proclaimed and ate a forkful of her omelet.

"I know," Michelle said, disappointed.

"Look at it this way, Michelle—God has everything under control," Liz reassured her best friend. "If He told you to wait on Him, then just wait on Him. Don't try and figure things out on your own, because it will never work out that way. Just trust God."

"I know. And I will. I guess I'm just going to have to give both brothas a rest for the time being. I need to figure out exactly what I want, but more importantly, what God wants for me. I need to figure out some things for myself—alone."

"Hey," Sandy said in a more chipper tone, "it's nothing

wrong with being alone. Look at me! I'm supersingle and free—and I'm doing all right!"

Liz and Michelle looked at each other and then let out a hearty laugh.

Sandy looked at the two of them as if to say, *What?* "Y'all crazy," she replied.

# Chapter 10

*Fill 'er Up!*

Sandy pulled out of the restaurant's parking lot only to discover her gas gauge for her royal-blue Neon was on E.

*Oh, great,* Sandy thought, *now I gotta go somewhere and find a gas station.*

Sandy eventually found a gas station, pulled up to a pump, paid with her debit card, then proceeded to pump unleaded gas into her tank. Upset that the handle on the gas pump didn't allow her to let go while the gas still continued to pump, since that part of the nozzle was broken, Sandy sighed, then kept pumping with her opposite hand on her hip as she looked around.

There were nothing but men at the gas station—two teenage boys entering the gas station's store wearing pants that hung below their belts, exposing their boxers, and one older gentleman walking back to his hooptie while talking on his cell phone.

She noticed a black Escalade on the opposite side of her and suddenly heard the blazing sounds of Byron Cage's version of "I Will Bless the Lord" booming outside the truck. It was rare that one heard gospel tunes coming out of a truck in this neighborhood, so Sandy peeked around to try and see who was disturbing the peace—or attempting to uplift the spirits of folks in the hood with their loud music.

As Sandy nearly broke her neck peeking around trying to see who drove the Escalade, she was startled by a raspy voice that seemingly crept up from behind her.

"Excuse me," the voice said as Sandy jumped in shock, busted.

She turned around and faced a very handsome man who looked to be about thirty-five. He was light skinned, about five-ten, and had a close haircut and a perfectly lined goatee that almost made him look like Chico Debarge. Sandy noticed he was carrying a can of pop instead of a forty-ounce—or a surprise drink in a brown paper bag. That was a plus. She peeked at his naked ring finger. Not married—another plus.

"Excuse me, miss, can you rub my chest?" the stranger asked.

"Excuse me?" Sandy asked, confused, with a half smile.

"Can you rub my chest?" he repeated.

"Can I do what? I'm sorry, sir, you must have me confused with some other chick. I don't get down like that," Sandy said and turned her back to him and continued to pump gas.

"No, I'm serious," the stranger continued.

Sandy started laughing, turned around to face him again and asked, "Why do you want me to...rub your chest?"

He held his chest with his free hand. "Because my heart hurts."

"Your heart hurts?"

"Yeah, my heart hurts. I need you to rub it and make sure it's okay, because my heart skipped a beat the moment I looked at you."

Sandy cheesed profusely. Of all the lines she had had thrown at her in her twenty-four years, she had never heard any brotha come up with a line that clever. She had to give it to him. That was definitely original.

Sandy laughed out loud. "Uh, thank you, I guess."

Just then the gas nozzle clicked, indicating Sandy now had a full tank. She was about to remove it when she was abruptly interrupted.

"Wait a minute, let me get that for you." The kind gentleman placed his can of pop on Sandy's car and then proceeded to take the nozzle out of the car and put it back in its place.

Sandy looked at him in amazement.

"I didn't want you to get your beautiful manicured hands all dirty," he said and then lifted her hand, the one that had just pumped gas.

"Your hands are so beautiful," he said in awe, complimenting her French manicure with its stencil design.

"They're almost as lovely as you," he said, then looked at her with his big brown eyes and long eyelashes. Sandy, for some reason, just loved men with long eyelashes.

"I'm sorry, I don't mean to be rude, my name is Jeremiah," he said and wiped his hand on his jeans, then extended it toward Sandy.

"Jeremiah?" Sandy repeated while still somewhat in a daze.

"Yeah, like the weeping prophet. Except I don't weep…at least not anymore."

"Not anymore?" Sandy asked with a concerned look on her face. "Why did you weep before?"

"Well, I wept about two weeks ago, when my girlfriend of two years broke up with me."

"Oh," Sandy said. "Why did she break up with you?" Sandy asked, since he apparently seemed pretty open about sharing his business with a stranger.

"She wanted to sleep with me, and I wanted to wait until we were married."

Sandy's ears perked up. She *must* be dreaming.

He continued, "She kept trying to seduce me, until finally I told her that I love God more than her and I couldn't let her keep trapping me like she was in order to take advantage of me."

"You poor thing!" Sandy cried and grabbed his hand, empathizing with the heavenly creature. "I'm so sorry to hear that, Chico—I mean, Jeremiah." Sandy had to catch herself.

"I don't know why I'm sharing all this with you anyway," Jeremiah said with lowered eyelids. "I'm sure you're in a serious relationship with someone right now. You're probably engaged."

"What makes you think that?" Sandy asked with a smile. She loved taking any opportunity to receive a compliment.

"A woman as fine as you? I'm sure you have all kinds of men beating down your door just to take you out."

Sandy considered Jeremiah's last statement and briefly thought about how the last man she was interested in didn't give her any compliments at all but instead gave her a two-dollar piano lesson and mean looks from a jealous boyfriend who envied her shoes. She laughed out loud as she remembered that scene from last night.

Jeremiah looked at her with a wide grin. "You have the most beautiful smile. Your teeth are so white. I can tell you really take care of yourself, young lady."

"Jeremiah, you're too kind," Sandy said in her best royal impression. "I can tell you're a really sweet person."

Jeremiah nodded in agreement.

"I just have one question for you. Have you received Jesus Christ as your personal Lord and Savior?"

"No doubt!" Jeremiah stood up tall and proclaimed loudly and proudly. "Jesus is my best friend! He's my Healer, He's my Provider, my Protector, my Everything! Hallelujah!" Jeremiah said while waving his right hand in the air. "Praise Him! Praise Him!" he shouted with a stomp, imitating someone in church about to catch the Holy Ghost.

Sandy cracked up laughing.

"See, there's that smile again," Jeremiah said while lightly lifting Sandy's chin. Sandy's smile turned solid as she stared deeply into his eyes, longing to kiss his full, pink, wet lips.

The chemistry was growing strong—a little too strong for Sandy to bear—so she proclaimed, "Look, Jeremiah, it was very nice meeting you, but I really have to get going."

She figured if he was going to ask her for her phone number, it was either now or never. If never, then she would prefer he just leave her well enough alone and let her go on her merry way.

"Wait a minute, beautiful. You didn't even give me your name?"

"Sandy," Sandy said, irritated, as she took a seat in her car with the window already rolled down.

"Sandy, let me take you out sometime. Can I give you a call?"

Sandy perked up. He wasn't just trying to get her digits to probably add to his collection, he wanted to take her *out*.

Sandy gave a smile, said "Sure" and jotted her number on the back of a white envelope.

"Mind if I call you tonight?" Jeremiah asked as he grabbed hold of Sandy's phone number like an eager four-year-old taking hold of a new toy.

"Tonight will be fine."

"Good. I want to make sure my angel makes it home safe and sound."

Sandy grinned lightly. Her father used to call her "angel" before he and her mom died in a car accident when she was just six years old. She was surprised that Jeremiah called her that.

"Well, it was nice meeting you, Jeremiah," Sandy said while taking one hand off the steering wheel and sticking it outside her car window.

"The pleasure was all mine," Jeremiah replied and then lightly grabbed her hand, softly kissed its palm, then looked back at her with a smile.

Sandy figured she better drive off right now before this man had her eating out of the palm of his hands.

*Mercy,* Sandy thought as she fiercely drove away.

# Chapter 11

*Pop Visit*

I had been sitting on my couch sipping hot tea with lemon, reading Jacquelin Thomas's *The Prodigal Husband* for the past two hours, when my apartment buzzer buzzed.

That's funny. I wasn't expecting any company.

I hit the talk button on the speaker and yelled, "Who is it?"

"It's me," a somewhat familiar voice responded. It was too deep to be David's. It couldn't be...

"Me, who?" I asked, not wanting to make a wrong assumption.

"It's Pierre, love. Let me in."

Pierre? I wasn't expecting him. I'm not in the mood for any pop-up, surprise visits right about now. Especially not from Pierre, the man God told me to put the brakes on. Although I hadn't quite gotten around to communicating that piece of information to him yet. For all Pierre knows, the two of us are still in the process of rekindling old flames.

I had to stop and think for a minute. *Should I let him in?*

Man, I wish I would've called him earlier to tell him we shouldn't see each other anymore. I was so engrossed in my novel and enjoying a Sunday evening alone in my apartment that I didn't feel like communicating with the rest of the world.

The buzzer sounded again.

"Just a second," I yelled in the buzzer, then rushed to the restroom to peek at myself in the mirror. I ferociously brushed my wrap style until it looked somewhat decent, applied a fresh coat of burgundy lipstick and black eyeliner and patted translucent powder all over my face—all in just two minutes.

Out of the bathroom, I tucked my Holy Hip-Hop T-shirt into my faded jeans, then hit the buzzer once again in order to let Pierre inside the complex.

I took a deep breath, exhaled, then opened the door and spotted Pierre looking as fine as ever in his black button-down shirt and blue jeans, walking down the hall to my apartment.

"It's about time you let me in," Pierre said as he stepped inside my place and attempted to give me a peck on the cheek. I held back to where he missed my cheek but instead kissed the air.

"Oh, now, there you go," Pierre said and pulled something from behind his back. It was two dozen red roses in a beautiful crystal vase.

"For me?" I asked in shock. I couldn't remember the last time David ever bought me a dozen roses, let alone two dozen.

"Of course they're for you. You're the only woman for me," Pierre said as a matter of fact.

"They're beautiful, thanks," I replied as I took the vase of roses and placed it in the center of my small yellow kitchen table. Roses always have a way of beautifying any room.

"I'm glad you finally decided to open the door for me. For a minute there I didn't think you were going to let me in," Pierre said with a slight cocky laugh.

"I wasn't," I said plainly.

Maybe rudeness will help him lose his attraction for me.

"What?" Pierre asked, confused.

"I wasn't going to let you in," I repeated with an attitude.

"Why not?"

"Pierre, I've got a lot on my mind right now and I know what I want, but I have to do what's right for me." *Lord, I hope this is coming out right.*

"But what's right for you is me, Michelle. Can't you see that?"

I paused, looked at Pierre, then admitted in a sincere tone, "I don't know, Pierre."

"What do you mean you don't know?" Pierre suddenly got loud and defensive. "Don't you think I have feelings, too?"

"I *do* think you have feelings, Pierre!" I proclaimed.

"What we shared last night—that was real, Michelle. That was the most peace I've felt in a long time, and I only feel that peace when I'm with you!" He sounded so sincere.

I couldn't take it anymore. I looked away because I couldn't face him any longer.

"And I can't imagine me coming all over here and you not wanting to let me in?" Pierre pleaded.

I attempted to avoid eye contact with him now at all costs because I didn't want him to see my eyes swell with tears.

*Why was he making this so hard?*

Pierre suddenly grabbed me and pulled me close. I could feel his breath on my neck. "Why wouldn't you let me in, Michelle?"

No words escaped my lips. He was firm yet gentle at the same time. He wanted what he wanted—and he wanted me.

Pierre spun me around and pinned me to the wall. I thought he was going to kiss me, but instead he pointed his finger to my chest and softly asked, "Why won't you let me in, Michelle?" His minty-fresh breath was soothing, as was his heartfelt plea.

"Why won't you let me into your heart?" he asked, then lowered his head in shame.

God knows I just wanted to rub my fingers through his hair and grab hold of him to let him know everything was going to be all right. God knows I wanted to kiss him for the rest of the night and tell him that I could be his forever. But God also knows that I received instructions from Him to let Pierre go for the moment, and now I'm face-to-face with the decision to trust that the God I serve knows what's best for me.

*But why, God, why?* I cried on the inside as this grown man laid his head on my chest like he was a helpless child.

"I'm sorry, Pierre," I said and softly pushed him away from me. "This is really hard for me, but I'm going to have to let you go now."

Pierre looked at me like a lost puppy.

"Pierre, I'm going to have to let you...out."

"But, Michelle—"

"Please don't make it any harder than it has to be, Pierre. I do have feelings for you, but we just can't be together right now," I attempted to rationalize.

"Why not?" Pierre demanded with a fierce, distorted look on his face. I didn't know he could look so mean.

I tried to remain calm. "You won't understand, Pierre. I appreciate the flowers, though. If you want, you can have them back."

Pierre suddenly screamed and swore at me. "I don't care nothing about no flowers! All I care about is you! I want *you*, Michelle!"

*Lord, should I call the police or something?* He was getting a little carried away. I had never heard Pierre swear before or look all wild and crazy like a maniac.

"Man, just forget it!" he shouted. "Have a nice life!" He walked out, then slammed the door so hard a picture of me and my family fell off my entertainment center and crashed onto the hardwood floor.

I put the picture back in its rightful place and thought to myself that maybe it was best that Pierre and I not pursue a serious relationship. Pierre obviously has a mean streak, and Lord knows I don't want to deal with that. Thank you, Lord.

# Chapter 12

*I've Got a Testimony!*

Liz and Matt Jr. took seats in the fifth row of Faith in Christ Church, Matthew's home church in the city. Men in white shirts and black ties scurried around as they unfolded several gray folding chairs on the hardwood floor in preparation for tonight's service.

Faith in Christ Church's own staff minister, Minister Matthew Long, was the guest speaker, as they normally have a different guest speaker during Sunday-night service. Liz wanted to make sure she arrived early so she could get a good seat up front so she could hear her man preach.

Liz decided against sitting in the very first row because she didn't want to be seen or seem like some people who just have to sit up front to feel important, so she figured the fifth row was okay, just enough so Matthew could see that she and her son were there for support.

Matt Jr. squirmed around in his chair as he waited for service to begin.

"When is Daddy going to preach?" he asked.

"He'll be on shortly, little Matt. Just hold on a minute," Liz added while patting little Matt's knee.

"Okay," Matt responded.

Liz was so amazed how Matt Jr. was such a well-mannered, well-behaved child. Though still a little boy who was very much active and enjoyed running around, wrestling with his dad and playing touch football, he still knew how to behave when he was in church. Stay seated and be quiet.

Liz tore off a sheet of her notebook paper and gave it to Matt, along with a red pen, so he could draw. She figured that would hold his attention until service began. Matt Jr. positioned his piece of paper on his lap, making sure not to mistakenly write on his khaki pants, and proceeded to doodle.

Ten minutes later a line of twenty people in royal-blue-and-white robes came marching down the center aisle singing "I'm Glad to Be in the Service" while clapping their hands to the beat played by a thirteen-year-old drummer positioned in the corner of the small stage up front.

As the choir proceeded down the aisle, everyone in their seats stood up, so Liz grabbed Matt's hand as the two of them stood up and sang along, as well.

Once the choir made their way to the stands, they ended their first song and then a heavyset woman stepped out of the choir stand and grabbed the microphone and bellowed, "I, I, I know I been changed!" The choir followed her lead as the soloist powerfully led the song as the congregation remained standing, and some of the members of the church waved their hands in agreement.

Once the choir was done with their A and B selections, an older, dark-skinned, bald-headed gentleman with gray hair protruding out the sides approached the pulpit wearing a bright yellow suit with matching yellow alligator shoes.

"Praise the Lord, saints!" Pastor Johnston proclaimed in a deep, raspy and authoritative voice.

"Praise the Lord!" the congregation replied, now filled with many church members fanning themselves profusely.

Pastor Johnston rustled through pages in his large King James Bible and then proclaimed, while still searching through his Bible, "I was glad when they said unto me, let us go into the house of the Lord."

"Amen," the church members said.

"We have a very special guest speaker tonight," the pastor continued. "Tonight we will be hearing the Word of God from one of our very own, Minister Matthew Long. Let's praise God as he comes."

The entire congregation gave a round of applause, and little Matthew shouted "Yay" as his father approached the pulpit as Pastor Johnston exited the stage and sat on the front row next to his wife, who wore a red St. John suit and large red church hat.

Matthew took a sip of water, which had been left for him on the pulpit, then smiled and said "Aah" as he set down

the refreshing drink. Snickers come from the congregation, as Minister Matthew Long is known to have a friendly,
personable personality, even from the pulpit.

"So how is everyone doing tonight?" the guest minister
asked.

A few people replied, "Fine."

Matthew repeated himself. "I said, how is everyone
doing tonight?"

"Fine!" More people responded, a little louder this time.

"Don't make me come out there now," Matthew proclaimed as he positioned his preaching Bible and notes on
the pulpit. Church members laughed out loud.

"Well let's dive on in." He began to pray, "Father, God, in
the Mighty, Matchless Name of Jesus, the Name that is above
every Name, I pray that you use me, Lord, to minister effec-
tively to your people. I pray that the words I speak will go
forth and land on good ground and will produce some
thirty-, some sixty- and some a hundredfold. I pray that I
decrease, and that You increase in me. In Jesus' Name,
amen."

"Amen!" the congregation shouted as folks began to sit
up straight in their seats, ready to receive an inspiring
Word from God.

"Today we're going to talk about fear," Minister Matthew
began from his notes. "God has not given us a spirit of fear
but of power, love and a sound mind."

Minister Matthew Long went on to preach about whatever
God has called you to do or whatever you feel God is leading

you to do, go ahead and do it. He went on to say that Satan is the author of fear, while God is the author of faith.

"I know of a young lady who recently received instructions from God to pursue full-time ministry," Minister Matthew continued.

Shocked, Liz looked around at the congregation, then back at Matthew. She wondered if he was talking about her.

"Well, instead of giving in to fear," he continued, "she is going to go ahead and quit her job and obey God."

Members of the congregation applauded.

"Now I'm not telling everybody to go ahead and quit your job because 'God told you to quit,'" Minister Matthew Long clarified. "You want to be sure you're hearing from God and that you're not just responding to that extra slice of pizza you had last night."

Members of the congregation laughed; however, Liz wasn't laughing at all. She felt somewhat embarrassed. How could he put her business out on the street like that?

By the end of his sermon, Minister Long had preached so hard that he'd had to continuously wipe his sweaty forehead with a white towel as church members had jumped out of their seats and shouted as he'd preached about how God has not given us a spirit of fear and how we can do all things through Christ. He'd preached from the very depths of his soul, so much so that there was barely a dry eye inside the small church building on the corner. Even so, Liz had decided that she still was going to have a word with Minister Matthew Long immediately after service.

# Chapter 13

As Sandy was about to pull up in her driveway, her cell ringtone of Kierra Kiki Sheard's "This is Me" went off, and she checked the caller ID. She didn't recognize the number, so she answered it.

"This is Sandra A. Moore. How can I help you?" she answered as she placed her car in Park and sat in the driveway.

"Hi, Miss Moore, this is Jeremiah. How are you?"

*Jeremiah?* Sandy thought. *He's definitely not shy about calling.*

"I'm fine," Sandy said. "Didn't I just talk to you, say, twenty minutes ago?"

"I know. I just wanted to make sure you made it home okay."

"Oh, that was extremely nice of you to check on me like that."

"Anytime. Don't you have something to ask me?"

"Like what?" Sandy asked, wondering what Mr. Jeremiah had up his sleeve this time. She was beginning to like this guy more and more.

"You should be asking me if my heart has recovered yet from its sudden interruption."

Sandy gave a hearty laugh. "You got me with that one, Jeremiah! Have you ever used that line on anybody else?"

"What anybody else? There is no one else! No one else has caused my heart to stop beating. What, you think I'm joking or something?"

Sandy was confused. She didn't know what to think and felt like dropping the whole conversation about the heart stuff.

After a brief pause, Jeremiah laughed in the phone. "I'm just messing with you, girl!"

"Oh!" Sandy said loudly into the phone with a slight laugh.

"Marcus, take that out your mouth!" Jeremiah yelled out of the blue.

*Who in the world was he yelling at?* Sandy thought.

"Sorry about that. My son was putting a dirty sock in his mouth. Kids."

"Oh, that's okay," Sandy said.

*So he has a son,* Sandy thought. *Hmm.* She'd never dated a man who had a child before. She knew Liz and Matthew were doing fine in their relationship, and he had a son, but Sandy never could see herself dating anybody with kids. Kids are just so nasty and sticky at times.

"You married?" Sandy asked. She just had to make sure.

"No, divorced," Jeremiah responded.

"Oh," Sandy replied in relief. Divorce is so common these days, so Sandy found that understandable. At least he'd married the woman he impregnated, even if it didn't work out, she concluded.

"Yup, I'm divorced. Covenant broken, but amen. I'm trying to move on with my life," Jeremiah said with a saddened tone.

"Was that the woman you were telling me about at the gas station, Weeping Prophet?" Sandy asked.

"Woman? Oh, her? No, that wasn't her. She was my first wife. I've been divorced twice."

"Twice?" Sandy yelled in the phone more loudly than she'd meant to. How much can she learn about this brotha in one sitting? She could maybe understand his being divorced once, but twice?

"Yeah, twice. I know it sounds like a lot."

*Um, yeah,* Sandy thought. Her dream man was turning into a nightmare on Elm Street.

"Enough of this. Why don't you let me tell you a little more about myself with you over dinner tonight?"

"Tonight?" Sandy asked. She wasn't quite sure if she wanted to go out with him, especially after she still heard little Marcus getting into more things he shouldn't be getting into in what sounded like the kitchen.

"Marcus, get your tail out of those pots and pans!" Jeremiah screamed outside the phone again. He came back to the phone. "I'm sorry, sweetheart. My boy just likes to get his hands into everything. You know how it is."

*No, I don't,* Sandy wanted to say but didn't. She really didn't know how to respond. Twice divorced with a bad kid?

"So can I pick you up at around seven? I have to drop Marcus off to his mom's upstairs and then head over to pick you up."

"Upstairs?" Sandy exclaimed.

"Yeah. I live in a two-family flat. We figured it'd be best for Marcus if we didn't live far away from each other. That way he can have access to either one of us at any time."

"Oh," Sandy said. *That makes sense,* she thought.

"So is it a date or what?"

"I don't know…." Sandy admitted in the phone.

"C'mon, I'll show you a good time. I would love to get to know you better and I would love to be able to stare into those crystal-blue eyes once more."

Sandy had forgotten she'd worn her blue contacts today. They must have really done the trick. But whether or not she was ready to go out with a brotha twice divorced, she still wasn't sure.

*What the heck,* she finally decided within herself. *If nothing else, I can get a free meal and a free night of some good eye candy. I'm not dating anybody, so I'm entitled to a little fun, right?* she rationalized. *One night out won't hurt, now, will it?*

# Chapter 14

*The Eleventh Woman*

Immediately after service, Liz gathered her large black-and-silver purse and Afrocentric Bible case and was about to take Matt Jr. with her up front in order to approach Minister Matthew Long when another young woman beat her to it.

Suddenly about ten people lined up after service to talk to Minister Matthew, as it is common practice for the guest minister to make himself available at the front to minister to the people and pray for them if necessary. However, Liz noticed that all of the patient prayer seekers were women—women who knew very well that Minister Matthew Long was an unmarried minister.

Instead of being the eleventh woman in line, Liz escorted little Matt up front and waited on the sidelines.

Liz figured everyone knows Minister Matthew has a son who is the spitting image of himself, so her taking hold of his hand in the front and on the side should give some of those man-seeking women some idea that this man of God just might be taken already.

"Minister Matthew Long!" the first girl said, brimming with excitement. Liz looked the chocolate-complexioned young lady with waist-length black zillions up and down as she noticed her short, tight black dress and sheer black stockings with a vertical line creeping up the back of her slim legs. Liz also couldn't help but notice her protruding belly. The girl, who didn't look a day over twenty-one, looked to be about six months pregnant.

"That was an awesome Word you preached today, Minister Long!" the young lady squealed.

"Thank you, my sister, thank you," Minister Matthew said warmly.

Liz couldn't remember ever seeing this young lady before, and the congregation was fairly small compared to her church.

*She must be new,* Liz thought, *right off the street.*

"I mean, that Word really hit home for me, especially since I've been going through a lot here lately," Liz heard the woman say, then stare at her own bun in the oven.

"I hear you," Minister Matthew responded sincerely. "You know what? Let's pray." Minister Matthew grabbed the young lady's hands and they bowed their heads as Minister Matthew began praying. Liz leaned in closer so as to hear what was being said, but after unsuccessfully being able to hear anything, she eventually bowed her head and silently prayed in the Spirit in agreement with whatever was being prayed.

After the heartfelt prayer, the young lady gave Minister Matthew a huge hug. Liz thought she saw her slip a small piece of paper in his back pocket, but Liz wasn't quite sure. Next thing she knew, the woman left and up stepped another young woman approaching Matthew, standing in the need of prayer.

By the time the fourth woman got her spiritual need met, Liz got tired of standing and waiting and she could tell even little Matt was getting bored with waiting around as he squirmed with his sweaty hand holding Liz's.

Liz was about to have a seat on the stage steps, as the ushers had uprooted all the folding chairs, when she was approached by an older yet classy, sassy woman wearing a sharp purple-and-silver suit and matching purple church hat. She resembled Minister Matthew's mother.

"How's my favorite grandbaby?" the woman asked as she approached little Matt, kneeled down in front of him, then opened her arms wide.

"Nana!" Little Matthew beamed as he leaped into his grandmother's arms. Matthew's mom looked so good at fifty-seven; she didn't look to be anybody's nana.

"Hi, Mrs. Long," Liz proclaimed. Liz was definitely glad to see her. She was getting tired of standing up front alone as she waited for Matthew to get a free moment to speak to her.

"Well, hello there, Miss Coleman," Mrs. Long said, now

with little Matt tightly squeezing her hand. "Congratulations on being called to full-time ministry!" she said. "Matthew told me you quit your job!"

*Yeah, you and the whole congregation,* Liz thought. *Who else did he tell, the Pope?*

"Thanks," Liz replied with a forced smile. "God is good."

"You got that right! All the time, baby!" Mrs. Long replied. "So how's my big boy?" Mrs. Long returned her attention to Matt Jr. as he gave his nana a big smile and replied with a boisterous, "Fine!"

"You know what?" Nana then stooped down to speak to her grandson face-to-face. "I just so happen to have your favorite food waiting on the stove for you at home," she said while tugging on his shirt collar. "Lasagna!"

"Lasagna?" Little Matthew jumped up and down. He just loved Nana's lasagna.

"Ooh, can I go home with you tonight?" little Matthew asked while ferociously patting Nana on her shoulder.

"Well, we're going to have to check with your father, but I'm sure that it won't be a problem," she said, then kissed him on the cheek and stood up straight once again.

Minister Matthew prayed for the last woman in line and approached his mom, Liz and his son with a big group hug.

"How are my two favorite ladies doing tonight?" he asked.

"Fine!" they sang on one accord.

Matt Jr. looked up, feeling left out.

"And how's my favorite champion?" Matthew asked his son, then gave him a high five.

"Fine, Dad," little Matt replied.

"Son, that was an awesome Word you gave tonight. I just love when you let the Lord *use* ya!" Mrs. Long said with a thump on Matthew's shoulder.

*"Wehl,"* Liz said, imitating Matthew's pastor with a smile.

"Matthew, I want to take Matt Jr. home with me tonight," Mrs. Long said.

"Can I go, Dad, can I?" Little Matt pleaded while looking up at his dad with dark brown, begging eyes.

"Aw, Mom, you don't have to do that," Matthew stated.

"I insist. I know how tired you can get after you've preached, plus I have some lasagna at my place with little Matt's name on it."

Matt Jr. looked up at his grandmother and licked his chops.

"Okay, I'll stop by later tonight and bring his school bag and school clothes for tomorrow," Matthew agreed. With that, he gave his mother a peck on the cheek and said, "Thanks, Mom. You're the best."

"You're welcome, baby," she said and walked away while holding little Matthew's hand as he walked with a skip in his step.

Matthew watched his mom walk off with his son, shook his head and told Liz, "Mom is something else, isn't she?"

"She sure is," Liz replied drily.

"So how's my Elizabeth Coleman tonight?" Matthew asked while shifting his focus to the other woman in his life. "Did you enjoy the service?"

"I did," Liz said. "It was, um, interesting, to say the least."

"Interesting?" Matthew asked with a suspicious look. "Uh-oh, what's wrong?" he asked.

"Nothing's wrong, I just thought it was interesting, that's all."

"Interesting in a good way or a bad way?"

"Oh, just interesting. We can talk about it later. Are you doing anything later tonight?"

"No, I was just going home to get some rest. Why?"

"Wanna go out to discuss over dinner?"

"Discuss what?"

"Matthew, I would rather not discuss it here," Liz said while looking around at the last set of people leaving the church.

"Okay, fine, we'll discuss it at dinner. But I'm not quite sure what we'll be discussing. But if you insist."

"I insist," Liz said.


Once Liz and Matthew placed their orders with the kind waitress at a nearby Coney Island restaurant, Matthew loosened his black silk tie, then scooted closer to the small yellow table in order to give Liz his full attention. "Okay, Liz, sweetheart, what's on your mind?"

"Oh, nothing."

"Come on, Liz, don't make me try and pry it out of you!" he jokingly said while reaching over the table and poking Liz in her side.

Liz cracked a smile. "Well, let's just say I was a little, um, disturbed with what was said during your sermon today."

"What?" Matthew asked, perplexed. "You didn't like the message?"

Liz spoke more slowly as she felt as though she were

walking on eggshells. "No, the message was good. Definitely anointed."

Matthew looked at her as if to say, *well, what is it then?*

"It's just that your illustration or example…"

"Yeah?" Matthew asked.

"I'd rather you not…use me in it."

"Oh! Is that what this is all about?" Matthew asked in relief. "Well, I thought it was okay since I didn't use your name," he rationalized.

"No, you didn't use my name." Liz nodded in agreement. "But people, for the most part, can probably figure it out."

"Oh. Well, I thought you would want to share your testimony. I was just using it as an example to show how you don't have to be bound by fear to do what God has called you to do."

"I understand that," Liz stated, still speaking slowly and barely making eye contact, "but I would prefer if you would leave me out of your messages. Yes, it is my testimony, but it should be my decision if I want to share it or not."

"Oh, I see," Matthew said. For the next few minutes the two of them were silent. The waitress brought their food and placed it on the table, and Matthew grabbed the ketchup and poured it on his fries.

"Matthew, look," Liz began to break the silence. "I didn't mean to hurt your feelings."

"You didn't hurt my feelings, trust me," Matthew said, agitated.

"Well, then, what is it? All of a sudden now you're all quiet on me."

"I'm quiet because I don't know what to say," Matthew said. "Lately you've just been acting so uptight, like I can't do anything right."

"That's not true," Liz concluded. "You do a lot of things right, like how you share your care and concern for other people in your congregation. Like how you're always willing to *pray* for other people."

"Well, thank you. At least I'm doing *something* right."

After a brief pause Liz suddenly looked up at Matthew and asked, "Did that woman give you her phone number?"

"What woman?" Matthew asked with a slight laugh, then threw his hands in the air in surrender.

"That woman you prayed for. The first one, the pregnant girl, did she slip you her phone number?"

Matthew nervously looked around the half-empty restaurant, then admitted, "Yes, she did."

Liz threw her fork on her plate and proclaimed, "I knew it!"

"You have to understand that I'm in the ministry," Matthew began. "I *have* to pray for people. And more than likely I end up praying for a lot of women. And some of them are so weak and confused that they look to me for guidance and consolation. This is my job. This is my calling. As the Lord promotes and exalts me where I will have my own church one day, I'm going to have to deal with women, even counsel them. And I'm also going to have to be on the road a lot, ministering in different churches across the country. So if I'm away, I can't have my wife sitting at home with my children thinking I'm out cheating on her with some other woman."

"What makes you think she's going to be sitting at home?" Liz asked sternly. He must have forgotten God had called her to full-time ministry, as well.

Matthew was at a loss for words. He continued softly, "Liz, I know more than likely my wife won't be just sitting at home. I realize that God may have a ministry call on her life, as well. But me and my wife will have to be together on this. We have to operate as a team. We have to flow in unison, and she's going to have to trust me. Liz, I'm going to need you to trust me on this. You *must* understand."

"I do understand, Matthew," Liz said, looking down at her hands placed firmly in her lap. She had barely touched her food.

Matthew sat back in his chair and released a sigh of relief.

Liz looked up at Matthew and asked, "But did you have to take it?"

"Take what?"

"*Her phone number!* Did you have to take it?"

Matthew threw his hands in the air again. "Now there you go again! What was I supposed to do? She walked off before I could give it back to her!"

"You could have taken it *out* of your pocket and given it right back to her right then and there. Now she's going to be looking for you next week wondering why you didn't call her!"

Matthew shook his head and took a bite of his deluxe cheeseburger.

"What?" Liz asked as a result of the silence. Now she was really agitated. *He just doesn't get it, does he?* she thought.

"Nothing," he said.

"What?" Liz insisted.

"I think this whole conversation goes far beyond some woman in church giving me her phone number."

"What do you mean?"

"You know what I mean," Matthew said accusingly.

Liz had no idea what Matthew Long was talking about. He was the fool, not her. Couldn't he see that?

# Chapter 15

*A Gift From Heaven*

"Angel, you look gorgeous!" Jeremiah proclaimed while hungrily eyeing Sandy, who sat across from him at the two-seat table in the dimly lit restaurant. She grinned, then used one hand to adjust the big pink satin bow attached to her shoulder on her one-sleeved black minidress. Sandy could remember buying this dress six months ago from off the clearance rack at her boutique, then partaking of the additional employee discount, which always came in handy. She was excited that she finally had somewhere to wear it. She'd decided to go heavy on the makeup tonight; she figured she hadn't gone out on a date in a long time, so she may as well look the part as much as possible.

"Thank you, Weeping Prophet," Sandy said. "You don't look too shabby yourself," she replied in reference to

Jeremiah's gray blazer with a black silk shirt underneath with its top three buttons undone revealing a somewhat hairy chest.

"I try," Jeremiah said and sat back and jokingly popped his collar. He grabbed his glass of Merlot, took a sip, licked his lips and asked, "So how do you like this spot?"

Sandy looked around the tiny, intimate restaurant she had never patronized. She noticed the set of drums, keyboard and microphone stands and figured a band would start performing soon. The bright orange candle in the center of the small table definitely helped the romantic ambience.

"It's nice," she replied while looking around at the other patrons, who seemed to be enjoying themselves. Everyone was pretty much coupled up.

"So how was Marcus when you left him?" she asked, hoping her inquiry of concern for his son would cause him to like her even more.

"Oh, he was doing fine," Jeremiah said. "Glad to be back in Mommy's arms. You know how that goes."

"Oh," Sandy said. "How old is he?"

"He's two."

"Oh, two!" Sandy said as if she'd received a sudden revelation. "That explains why he's getting into everything! You know what they say about those two-year-olds!"

"Oh, yeah—terrible twos. I forgot about that."

The two of them laughed.

"He's still a little more active than my other son was when he was two, though," Jeremiah said.

"Your other son?" Sandy inquired with a tilted neck.

"Yeah. My other son, Micah. Micah's four now, but when he was two he was a lot quieter than Marcus."

*How many kids does this man have?* Sandy thought. She couldn't take it any longer. It was time to get the lowdown on this man; what is *really* going on?

"How many kids do you have, Jeremiah?" Sandy asked and took a sip of her cranberry juice on the rocks.

Ever since her almost-fatal incident with Carter, Sandy had taken a vow to never drink another glass of alcohol again. She couldn't trust herself at all after that incident.

"Five," Jeremiah said coolly.

"Five!" Sandy exclaimed and almost choked on her drink.

"Yeah, five. Three boys and two girls," he replied like a proud dad.

Sandy was too outdone. She was about ready to ask for the check and catch a cab back home.

"Um, what are their ages?" Sandy asked—as if she really cared at this point.

"Let's see...twenty, seventeen, thirteen," Jeremiah began, counting on his fingers. "Uh, four and two."

"Whoa, that's a lot of kids!"

"Yup. Madison, Melanie, Margie, Micah and Marcus."

"Well, my, my, my," Sandy said and drained the rest of her cranberry juice. Even though she'd vowed not to drink again, at this point she was ready to ask for a shot of something.

"Three from my first marriage and two from my last marriage."

"And you're how old?" Sandy just had to know.

"Thirty-six. I had my first child while I was in high school. I was young and dumb, ya know."

*And extremely fertile, obviously,* Sandy thought.

"But I'm different now. I got saved two years ago, after my last child, and now I'm ready to turn my life around!"

"Oh," Sandy replied.

Jeremiah continued and grabbed Sandy's hand from across the table. "You know what, angel? I prayed for a woman like you."

*I bet you did,* Sandy thought and rolled her eyes in the back of her head.

He continued, "You know how the Bible talks about Abraham's servant in the book of Genesis, how he went out to look for a wife for Isaac and how the servant asked God for the woman who offers him water and also offers water to his camels to be a sign that she is to be Isaac's wife?"

"Uh-huh," Sandy responded, her crystal-blue eyes staring into his, praying he would get to the end of this story real quick so she could figure out a way to hightail it out of there.

"Well, that's kinda how it was when I met you," said the fertile prophet.

"Excuse me?" Sandy asked.

"Just before I met you at the gas station, I was in my truck, talking to God. I said, 'God!' I said it just like that, I said, 'God, I'm tired of being alone! I'm tired of messing up and picking the wrong ones over and over again. I'm ready to get it right this time!' That's exactly what I said just before I met you. The third time will definitely have to be a charm for me." Jeremiah scooted closer in his seat and looked Sandy dead in the eye. "I said, 'God, when I go to this gas station, if I see a woman who is five-two, light-skinned with short black hair, and if I find out she loves the Lord and smiles at me real big, then I'll *know* she's the one for me!' Now how tall are you?"

"Uh, five-four," Sandy lied. She wasn't about to tell this weirdo that she was really five-two. He was turning out to be a little too spooky for her taste.

"Oh, really? You look five-two to me. But, anyway, that's beside the point. I know a good thing when I see it, and you, Miss Sandra A. Moore, are definitely a good thing. You my missing rib, girl!"

Sandy laughed lightly as if to say, *Why, God, why?*

"Sandy, not to pry, but how is your medical history?" the prying prophet asked.

"I'm sorry, what did you say?" Sandy asked, perplexed. Did he just ask what she thought he just asked?

"Do you have any STDs? I mean, since I believe you might be wifey and all, I have to check up on these things, ya know."

"Excuse me," Sandy said and threw her white cloth napkin on the table and made a mad dash to the ladies' room. She had had enough of this nonsense.

Inside the restroom, Sandy washed her hands and took a few moments to compose herself.

Sandy returned to her seat only to notice the lights were even dimmer and that the band had begun playing a smooth jazz groove.

*This is perfect,* Sandy thought, relieved. She sat down

without even giving Jeremiah a second look and faced the band while swaying right along with the music.

After two songs, Sandy was actually starting to enjoy the four-member ensemble and even thought the bass player was kinda cute with his husky build, mahogany-brown skin, dented bald head and dangling earring, which made him look like a pirate. She figured she might as well focus all of her attention on this man since she and Mr. Weeping Prophet were obviously bound for nowhere.

Jeremiah accusingly stared at Sandy with his elbows on the table and his hands locked together. The scented candle in the center of the table flared as Jeremiah stated loudly, "Nice band, huh?"

"Huh?" Sandy asked, acting as though she didn't hear a word he'd just said.

"I said nice band!" Jeremiah yelled.

"Yeah, real nice!" Sandy replied, keeping her eye on the bassist.

Jeremiah called the waiter over and whispered something in his ear and placed a bill in his hand. The waiter then made it to the band in the front and whispered something in the ear of the lead soloist, who was a sultry woman wearing a slinky silver slip dress with spaghetti straps that loosely hung off her shoulders.

The band finished their last song, received hefty applause. Then the soloist spoke into the microphone.

"Thank you, thank you, thank you all," the soloist said as she scoped the entire restaurant. "You all are too kind," she said in a deep, mellow voice. "This next song

I'd like to dedicate to a person this man says is the most beautiful, alluring and angelic woman in the room, Miss Sandra A. Moore."

Everyone clapped as Sandy looked around, startled to hear her name called. She looked over at Jeremiah, who gave her an assuring nod with his hand underneath his chin.

The band started to play and the soloist began to moan into the microphone and passionately rock from side to side. "Ooh ooh ooh ooh ooh ooh," she sang and then began singing the first verse to Anita Baker's "Angel."

Sandy didn't know what to make of her Weeping Prophet's sincere, romantic gesture. She was speechless. A song dedicated especially for her? "Angel" at that? How sweet! She had never had anyone do anything so thoughtful for her!

As the soloist continued to sing the song almost as well as Ms. Baker herself, Sandy felt like crying as she thought about how her father used to tuck her in bed at night and say, "Good night, my sweet angel."

Sandy's fond memory was interrupted by Jeremiah standing over her and placing his hand out toward her.

"Care to dance, angel?"

Sandy looked up and thought she saw her father staring back at her, then she shook herself and saw Jeremiah's strikingly handsome face. She obligingly took his hand as he led her out to the empty dance floor.

Jeremiah held her close and rubbed his hands up and down her back as he rocked her like a father cradling a newborn. He blew softly in her ear and whispered something Sandy could barely comprehend.

Sandy closed her eyes and envisioned her own father rocking her back and forth, just as he used to do when she used to have trouble sleeping as a child. She laid her head on Jeremiah's broad shoulder and smiled.

So what that Jeremiah wasn't exactly the man that she wanted him to be? So what that Jeremiah wasn't exactly her father, whom she missed so dearly and who was probably peeking at her right now from heaven? Tonight Jeremiah was all the man that Sandy needed at this very moment, even if it was all just a dream.

# Chapter 16

*Peace Be Still*

"Yaaaaaaaawn!" I proclaimed as I lifted from my twin bed and gave a wide stretch. "Michelle, girl, it's time to get up," I said to myself. I crawled out of bed at six-ten on this lovely Monday morning. I showered, put on my corporate navy-blue pant suit, grabbed a breakfast bar, my navy-blue leather purse, slim-line Bible and journal and headed out the door to attend morning prayer service at church.

Once inside the sanctuary, I found my usual spot in the corner, where I set my things and immediately lifted up my hands in order to thank God for His many blessings. I was definitely thankful for my latest promotion on the job, as I am no longer a Human Resources generalist but now have the honor of being called an HR Manager at Lasek Automotive Supply company's corporate headquarters.

Though I had been in that position for the past two months, I was still getting used to the concept of people having to report to me, versus the other way around. My previous boss, Susan, got relocated to a plant in Florida.

I was praising God as soon as I found that out three months ago, because Susan had been known to give me many a headache at any given moment on the job.

Soon after she left, I willingly and voluntarily stepped up my game and took on her previous responsibilities as HR Manager as well as took care of my own responsibilities, at the time, as a generalist. My hard work, stamina and innovative ideas gained the attention and favor of the vice president of the company, Bob Nash, who offered me a promotion only a month after Susan's departure. So now instead of a small cubicle in the corner, I am flying high in my new corner office with a huge window overlooking the downtown landscape of the city.

After thanking and praising God for a few minutes right along with the rest of the congregation, the female minister led prayer, and I made my way in the aisle to walk around and pray in the Spirit in agreement with the minister. I kept my eyes open as I prayed, since I didn't want any head-on collisions in the church house, and couldn't help but notice a familiar face praying fervently on the opposite end.

He wore a bright red T-shirt and black slacks. His height and extreme good looks made him stand out from the crowd. The man I hadn't seen at early-morning prayer in the last year and a half is now here once again, praying like Jesus is about to make a surprise guest appearance today.

To be honest, I wasn't sure about Pierre's motives for re-appearing at early-morning prayer. I agree that everyone has a right to pray in the midst of the saints, but it sure was funny how Pierre always seemingly and suddenly reappeared in the sanctuary this early anytime he was trying to regain my attention.

I had determined then and there that as soon as the minister dismissed everyone, I was going to dart out of that sanctuary like a thief in the night.

After praying for an hour, I made it back to my seat, and the minister opened her Bible to recite the scripture of the day.

"Saints," the young minister stated, "today's scripture is found in Isaiah 26:3, which reads, 'Thou wilt keep him in perfect peace whose mind is stayed on Thee, because he trusteth in Thee.'" I jotted down the scripture, nodded my head, then shot a look at the back door.

"Let's give the Lord a shout of praise as we commit to keeping our minds on Him today!" the minister lifted her hands and shouted. I shouted, as well, and also gathered my things and shouted my way all the way to the back near the exit.

As soon as the minister said, "You are dismissed," I dashed out of that back door so fast you would think I left skid marks on the pavement.

Once outside, I turned around and breathed a sigh of relief as, after a few minutes, I didn't notice Pierre following after me. He must have gotten caught speaking to someone else. Nonetheless, I was thankful to God I didn't have to face him once again.

I praise God for the strength to tell him no last night, even though my flesh wanted to tell him yes. My soul wanted to tell him yes. My body wanted to tell him yes. So help me, God.

The closer I got to my blue Taurus, I noticed something on its windshield. Whatever it was, it was red and it had a white piece of paper attached to it. As I got a few feet away from my car I discovered that it was a single long-stemmed rose positioned underneath one of my windshield wipers, with a folded note attached.

I grabbed the note which read: *As I left your place last night, I found this rose on the hall floor on my way out. I must have dropped it on my way to your apartment door. Nonetheless, I wanted to make sure you had it. Now your bouquet is complete. I know how much you love red roses, so I wanted to make sure they were perfect and beautiful, just like you. Have a wonderful day in Christ. PD*

"Why, God, whyyyy?" I cried in my car as I set the rose and note on the seat beside me, then turned the ignition key and headed to work.

I felt like throwing a temper tantrum right inside my ride. Lord knows I love the Lord with all my heart, with all my mind and with all my strength, but sometimes I just wonder, is all this waiting stuff really worth it?

I decided then and there to have a special talk with God later tonight.

I was amazed that I was able to accomplish anything today at work, let alone complete five things on my to-do list right before lunchtime. It definitely helps now that I have an assistant, Niki, to help me get some of this work done. I was able to delegate over half my projects to her. I don't know what I'd do without that girl. One day I'm going to have to treat her to lunch or something, because she definitely does a great job at helping make me look good.

After sipping the last of my third cup of caramel latte, I received an internal call from the receptionist.

"Hello?" I replied.

"Michelle, I have a gentleman up front by the name of Pierre Dupree who would like to see you."

*Pierre?* "Tell him I'm not here," I blurted without giving it a second thought. Hopefully he didn't hear me through the phone.

"Uh," the receptionist, Debra, continued hesitatingly, "he actually has some things with him."

*Things, what things? More flowers? More notes? Can't this man take a hint? He's only making it harder for the both of us.*

"Tell him I don't want it…tell him I've already left for lunch," I replied. *Okay, Lord, I apologize for lying, but I had to think of something!*

"Uh…" Debra continued, not hanging up the phone or passing on any of the things I'd just said to her to Pierre.

"What is it, Debra? Did you hear what I just said?"

"Uh," Debra said one last time and finally decided to say what was on her mind. "He kinda brought lunch—"

"So!" I didn't care that he'd brought me lunch. No means no, and that's it! He can't win me over with food. Besides, I'd brought my own lunch from home.

"Not for just you," Debra explained, "for the whole department."

"For the whole department? What do you mean?" I asked.

Debra drew the phone closer to her mouth and spoke quietly and excitedly. "Girl, this man brought bags full of submarine sandwiches, cookies, chips, water and pop! This man brought lunch for *everybody!*"

*Just great.* How can I turn down a benevolent gesture like that which benefits not only just me but the entire staff? The entire, obviously hungry staff, as indicated by Debra's sense of urgency and willingness to not allow him to be turned away. Turning him away will only make me look like the bad guy. However, accepting his gesture will make him look like a hero. Slick move, Mr. Dupree.

"Let him in." I gave in. I had to.

Niki opened my door and in walked suave, smooth and sophisticated Mr. Pierre Dupree himself, all suited up, looking more like he was about to be interviewed for a job here instead of someone who just happened to stop by with brown grocery bags filled with the works, just like Debra had indicated.

"You can just set them on the desk over there. I'll make an announcement to the staff that the food is here once you're gone," I said drily and remained seated.

Pierre set down the bags and gave me a weird look. "Baby, aren't you glad I blessed your staff with a free meal?"

"Pierre," I started while remaining seated, not offering him a seat. "First of all, I'm not your baby. And second of all, I don't need any of your handouts. What's the *real* reason you just decided to 'bless' my team today? Huh?"

Pierre was silent for a few minutes as he looked down at his own manicured hands.

I looked at him with my head cocked to the side, wondering when he would decide to answer me. I wished it was soon, because I needed to tell these hungry employees they have food waiting for them before they decided to go out and buy their own lunches. Then again, knowing Debra, she had probably e-mailed and called everyone already, letting them know that lunch is on the house today, compliments of Michelle's ex-boyfriend.

"I'm waiting," I said, tapping the desk with my fingertips.

"I miss you, Michelle," he said while looking up at me. I must admit, those hazel eyes were working their magic once again. "I miss having you in my life," he admitted. "I miss your laugh, I miss your smile."

I cracked a smile. At least he was being honest.

"I messed up," he continued. "I know I messed up. But I want to make it up to you." Pierre leaned in closer to me. "I know I'm not perfect, Michelle. I realize I made a mistake. Lots of times. I apologize for flying off the handle and getting all loud and crazy on you last night." Well, at least he recognized he was wrong for going off on me.

He continued, "I want you back, baby—I'm sorry, I mean Michelle Lashay Williamson."

This time I looked at my own French-manicured nails positioned in my lap.

Next thing you know, I heard his low, baritone voice

delicately enunciate those three small yet powerful words—"I love you."

There he goes again. Reciting those three words every woman wants to hear and feel.

Those three words every woman wants to feel deep down in her soul and believe they're real.

"I love you, too, Pierre." I'd released those words out of my mouth quicker than I could even take them back.

To be honest, once I'd said it I felt a sense of freedom come over me. I was finally free to express how I truly felt about him. No reservations. No inhibitions. Just freedom, from the heart.

Pierre hopped up from his seat and came around my desk, lifted me up and gave me a huge, tight hug. He kissed me on the cheek and squeezed me tightly once again.

I hugged him back, wiped a single tear before it left my eye, then released myself from his grasp to look at him face-to-face.

He suddenly looked at me like he didn't know what was wrong—like he wondered why I had freed myself from his embrace.

I looked deep into his eyes and said, "I do love you, Pierre." He gave me a soft kiss on the lips.

Lord knows I wanted to return his short, soft kiss with another one of my own...and another one and another one. It just felt so right being in his arms again. But I couldn't let it go on like this. I had to do what was right.

"But I love God more," I finally admitted.

Pierre looked at me like I'd just stabbed him in his chest.

"What?" He shoved me away and I fell back a few feet, tripping over my heels and almost running into the desk behind me.

I hadn't realized Pierre was so strong. I couldn't believe he'd just pushed me!

"I'm sorry, Pierre," I said, stumbling to regain my balance, "but nothing's changed." I was starting to shake. "We can't be together."

"What do you mean?" Pierre asked hopelessly. "You just told me you loved me!"

"I do!" I admitted. I guess my admitting my love for him won't make him go away, but I had to be honest with him—and with myself.

"Then why can't we be together?" Pierre couldn't understand.

"It's not that simple, Pierre," I tried to explain. "We need to give it some time."

"Time? How much time do you need?" He raised his voice about ten decibels. "You can't put a hold on love! What we have is real, Michelle, and you keep wanting to throw it all away!"

"Pierre, you have to understand, I—"

"You know what?" Pierre threw his hands in the air in surrender. "That's it. I'm sick of this! I'm tired of playing these games with you, Michelle. I give you my heart, I try to be honest, and what do you do? You tell me you love me, then in the same breath tell me you don't want to be with me? Look, I'm sorry that I'm not perfect. What do you want, Jesus in a suit?"

"No, Pierre…"

"'Cause I'm not Him!" he yelled even louder. "I'm just a man who loves you so bad that it hurts, Michelle, it hurts!" Pierre beat his chest with his fist as nosy coworkers peeked through the glass windows.

I spoke quieter so as to not draw any more extra attention to my office. "I know, Pierre. I know. Unfortunately now is not the time or the place—"

"You know what, Michelle?" Pierre pointed his finger at me. "There will never be a time or place better than right now. And right now you lost this, baby. I'm out. I'm through with this. I'm done for good. There's nothing else I can say or do."

"Pierre, if you like I can have my assistant escort you out the—"

"You know what?" Pierre asked, then hollered at me and told me where to go.

He then stormed out of my office and slammed the door like a madman.

I wasn't sure if I should call security or not. Instead I plopped in my seat, waited about five minutes, then called the front desk.

"Debra," I said coolly.

"Yes?"

"Did Mr. Dupree leave the building?"

"Yes, he did."

"Good. Can you have maintenance bring extra plates and napkins? I'm going to need help setting this stuff up in the kitchen for the employees to enjoy their lunch."

"Okay, great," Debra said cheerfully and hung up the phone.

I buried my face in my hands, then rubbed my temples with my fingertips. I blinked my eyes several times so no tears would form, blew into a Kleenex, then grabbed my compact from my purse to touch up my powder and mascara, stood up, straightened out my suit, then proceeded to take the grocery bags to the kitchen in the back.

I tried my best to ignore the stares from coworkers. I hadn't meant for them to get a glimpse of my personal life. I'm sure this incident will be the talk of the town at the watercooler tomorrow morning.

Oh, well.

Even though Pierre turned my initial Spirit-filled day into seemingly a day sent by Satan himself, I can at least accept Pierre's gesture as a way to put smiles on the faces of the many employees who work here every day, who I'm sure have more serious problems than what I currently have to deal with.

For the rest of this day I chose to keep my mind on Jesus, because Lord knows right now I am in need of perfect peace.

# Chapter 17

*When God Calls*

"Okay, kids, I want us all to gather around and meet me in the circle near the play area," Liz told her second-graders at Bakersville Christian Academy as they finished coloring pictures they'd drawn of people they admire most. "Bring your pictures with you!" Liz stated in a loving tone as she headed toward the center of the classroom.

"Lord, give me strength," she whispered under her breath, as she was about to let her beloved students know that today was her last day of being their teacher since she'd decided to answer the call to full-time ministry.

Liz Coleman grabbed the chair in the middle of the floor, and the twenty students nicely sat on the floor in a big circle around her.

"Kids, I have an announcement to make."

All of the students suddenly got quiet and listened attentively. Some of them sat on their hands and arose in their seats.

*Okay, Lord, here goes,* Liz thought.

"I know you all love the Lord, and I love Him, too. And I feel that God wants me to do some things for Him, which includes being a minister for Him."

"You mean like a preacher?" Serena raised her hand and asked.

"Well, yes, sorta like that," Liz continued.

"Oh, wow, cool!" Dean proclaimed.

"But," Liz continued, "that means I won't be able to be a teacher anymore, so today is my last day with you guys."

Everyone was silent for thirty seconds, until Regina proclaimed, "Oh, no! You leaving us?"

Moans and groans were heard all over the room.

"In a way I am, I guess. I won't be your teacher anymore, but I'll always be your friend." Liz couldn't think of anything else to say.

"No, you won't! You leaving me! You just like my daddy!" Regina proclaimed and then angrily folded her arms.

"I'm sorry, kids." Liz was about to cry when little Dean walked up to her and patted her on the back.

"That's okay, Miss Coleman. We'll be fine," he said. And then he addressed the class. "Y'all should be happy for Miss Coleman! She's going to be a preacher man—I mean preacher woman!"

Some of the students perked up. Dean continued, "She's going to tell the world about Jesus! And we all need Jesus!" Some of the students nodded their heads in agreement.

Dean addressed Liz once again, "When I grow up, Miss Coleman, I want to be just like you!" Liz looked up at her miniature preacher man and gave him a big hug. All of the students followed and gave her another group hug. Liz was overcome with love.

# Chapter 18

*Picture Perfect*

"Sandra Moore, darlink, your sales for this month so far look absolutely wonderful!" Mrs. Boosler ranted and raved as Sandy organized the women's clothing rack at Braxton's department store, where Sandy was the assistant manager. She smiled wildly as Mrs. Boosler, her older, Caucasian boss and manager, gave her a big hug and a kiss on her cheek.

Mrs. Boosler, who was shorter than Sandy, with short white hair, reminded Sandy of a TV grandmother who was always ready to shower her grandchildren with love and milk and cookies. She was definitely ten times nicer and more understanding than Sandy's former boss, Geneva, who seemingly picked on Sandy for every little thing she did wrong.

Though Mrs. Boosler was a very sweet woman with a peaceful demeanor, she was very powerful. Her son-in-law,

Ted Braxton, owned the entire department store chain. Mrs. Boosler, at her age, really didn't have to work but could just live off her daughter and son-in-law. But instead of staying at home being unproductive, she'd decided she'd rather be out in the workforce, where she could be most useful and appreciated.

"Thank you, Mrs. Boosler! You're too kind." Sandy just loved her new boss. After a smooth transition from the six-month management training program, Sandy was elated once Mrs. B—as Sandy called her sometimes—decided she was ready to be entrusted with the duties and responsibilities of being an assistant manager.

Besides the extra hours she might work when she was closing or working extra hours during the holidays, Sandy absolutely loved her new job. She loved the discount she received on the fashionable new trends, her clientele and the nice salary increase, which included commission when she exceeded the goal for any given month.

"Whatever you want me to do for you, you let me know, okay?" Mrs. Boosler stated and walked to the back room.

Just then a short, brown-skinned, overweight man with a beige suit, beige hat and matching gold alligator shoes entered the store. He made his way to where Sandy was standing and pondering about Mrs. B's offer, then tapped her on the shoulder.

"Excuse me, miss, do you work here?"

Sandy turned around and looked the man up and down. "Yes, I do," she said.

"Good. Well, uh, maybe you can help me out. I'm

looking for an outfit for my niece, so I guess I'm looking for the junior department?"

Sandy flashed a warm smile. "Well, you're in the right place. That's my department!"

"I sure am glad of that, Praise the Lord," he said with a wave offering, then looked Sandy up and down.

"Praise Him. You're a believer, I take it?" Sandy asked. She was always excited about meeting other members of the fold.

"Oh, I believe, all right," he said while staring at Sandy, then shook himself. "I mean, yes, I'm a believer. I love the Lord with all my heart. I'm sorry." He removed his hat and placed it over his heart. "I haven't introduced myself properly. My name is Humphrey. Pastor Joseph Humphrey," he said and stuck out his free hand.

*Ooh, a pastor!* Sandy thought.

She had never dated a pastor before and always wondered what that would be like. Would he pray throughout the whole thing? Or would the two of them exchange stories about church members and some of their issues and drama?

At that moment she wished she'd worn her long, white, loosely fitting floral dress, instead of the fitted hot-pink sundress with orange flowers all over it with matching orange pumps. She must have missed God this morning as she'd thought about what to wear to work today.

Even though the vision which stood before her wasn't exactly her type physically—the belly which hung out over his pants didn't help the situation either—Sandy was always curious about dating a man with such power and authority.

"And your name is…" the pastor continued, still holding on to her hand.

Sandy shook herself back into reality and snuck a peek at his ring finger.

*No wedding ring. Yes!*

"I'm sorry. My name is Sandra A. Moore. It's a pleasure to meet you, Pastor Humphrey."

"The pleasure's all mine," the pastor said and kissed the hand he seemingly refused to let go.

The more charmingly he responded and the more he spoke with his deep, baritone voice, which reminded Sandy of the voice of God, the more attractive he became to Sandy. He slowly but surely was becoming her next assignment as she hung on every word he said.

Sandy was determined to win a date with this pastor. She wondered how many members were in his congregation.

"Now what is it that I can help you with, Pastor—even though you look as if you don't need *any* help," Sandy said with a sexy smile. "Besides the Lord's help, of course," Sandy added to include a spiritual twist to her flirtatious attempt.

"Ah, a virtuous woman," Pastor Humphrey concluded. "Sandy, I don't mean to be too forward, but do you have any plans for lunch this afternoon? That is, after I purchase my niece's birthday outfit?"

Saved, considerate, not cheap, seeing as he's shopping here at Braxton's, *and* he remembers birthdays—all pluses in Sandy's book.

But she still wanted to make sure of one thing.

"Got any kids?" she asked the pastor. Since he looked to

be well over forty, Sandy wanted to make sure he didn't have any kids who were almost as old as she was. Then again, that may be a plus since more than likely they'd be grown and already out the house.

"No, I don't have any kids. I'm widowed, and my wife and I never had any children," he replied with lowered eyes.

"Oh, sorry to hear that," Sandy said, yet she was still glad that he didn't have a starting lineup for a basketball team like her former Mr. Weeping Prophet.

Sandy suddenly had an "aha!" moment. She figured out how Mrs. Boosler could reward her for her stellar sales performance this month.

"Please wait right here a moment, Pastor Humphrey."

"Oh, I'll wait," the pastor said. "I'm not going anywhere," he added with gleaming eyes piercing Sandy's.

Sandy rushed to the back room in her heels and yelled, "Mrs. B! Mrs. B!"

"What is it, Sandy?" Mrs. Boosler asked, hoping nothing was wrong.

Out of breath, Sandy stated, "I figured out how you can reward me for my performance this month."

"Oh, really. How?" she asked.

"You can let me have the rest of the afternoon off."

Sandy stepped one foot inside Pastor Humphrey's long, shiny black Lincoln Town Car, got a whiff of its new-car smell, made herself comfortable in the soft beige interior leather seats and exhaled.

"Pastor Humphrey, you have a beautiful ride!" she exclaimed as she ran her fingers across the leather seats. "It's so roomy!" Sandy said as she peeked at the backseat.

"Thank you, thank you. God is good."

"All the time," Sandy said. "So how long have you been a pastor?" Sandy began as they began their journey to a museum, which was adjacent to a restaurant they were headed to for lunch.

"Oh, I've been a pastor for just two years. I'm pretty new at this."

"You're new at this?" Sandy asked. "And you got this Lincoln already?" Sandy hadn't meant to say that out loud.

Pastor Humphrey looked over at Sandy and said, "I didn't get the Lincoln with the church's money, in case you were wondering. I also own my own business on the side."

"Oh, really? Sounds exciting! What do you do?" Sandy was curious. She thought all pastors were just pastors and didn't have time for anything else.

"I'm in the global trade industry."

"Ooh," Sandy said as if she knew what that meant. The word *global* did have a nice, rich-sounding ring to it, though. "Where is your church located?" Sandy asked.

"On Temple Street. Since I'm just starting out, we hold service in my basement for now."

"In your basement?" Sandy asked. She thought all pastors had actual church buildings.

"Yes. Every Sunday for the past three months we've had service in the basement. Did you know the first church in the New Testament was held at someone's house?"

"Oh, well, no, I didn't. How many members do you

have?" Sandy wondered how many parishioners could fit downstairs.

"Right now, since I'm just starting out, four."

"Four? You only have four members?"

*Was this a church or a Bible study?* Sandy thought.

"Yes, four. The Word says where two or three are gathered together, Jesus is in the midst. So right now my church consists of me, my mother and my sister."

Sandy did the math in her head and couldn't figure it out. "But I thought you said you had four members?"

"The fourth member is Jesus!" Pastor Humphrey proclaimed. "But enough about me. What about you, Miss Sandra A. Moore? Do you do anything else besides work in the department store?"

"I sing in the choir at my church!" Sandy said proudly.

"Nice. So you sing?"

"I sure do. The choir director, Minister Brown, says I have the voice of an angel," Sandy replied.

Minister Brown actually gave that accolade to the entire choir one day during rehearsal, so Sandy decided to receive that compliment as her own. She might not have the best voice in the world, but she could carry a tune—so long as she wasn't forced to sing a solo.

"Well, that's great, Miss Moore. I'm sure our church can use a fresh voice to lead songs in our choir."

Pastor Humphrey pulled his car into a parking lot near the door of a museum with the adjacent café.

"After you, madam," he said and opened Sandy's car door for her.

*Madam?* Sandy thought. She hadn't heard anyone call her that in a long time. She wondered just exactly how old he was. With his thick mustache and hair that showed a hint of gray, he looked to be about forty-five.

Sandy and Pastor Humphrey grabbed a seat at a small table inside the modest restaurant. The wooden table and chairs were so small Pastor Humphrey kept fidgeting in his seat in order to get comfortable.

"I figured we'd eat here first, then head over to the museum afterward. Do you like artwork?" he asked.

"Oh, I love art," Sandy said as she grabbed her menu from off the table. "My favorite class in grade school was Art."

"Oh, I see. Who are some of your favorites? Picasso? Vincent van Gogh?"

"Um, I like them both. Oh, and I really like that Michael Tangelo guy."

"Michael Tangelo?" pastor asked, confused. "Do you mean, Michelangelo?"

"Yeah, him. I really like him. His stuff looks really nice. I heard he has an album coming out soon, too."

"Oh, really?" Pastor Humphrey said. "But Michelangelo died in the 1500s."

"Oh," Sandy said, slightly embarrassed. "Well, I must be getting him confused with someone else. So what are you going to order?" she asked in an attempt to quickly change the subject.

"I think I'll order the Reuben."

"Sounds good to me! I think I'll order that, too," Sandy proclaimed as she closed her menu.

Here lay the perfect opportunity to show that she could be the picture-perfect, submissive preacher's wife.

A cheerful blond waitress came and took their orders.

"Ladies first." The pastor motioned to Sandy.

Sandy just smiled and said, "I'll have what you're having."

The waitress and the pastor looked at each other, and Pastor Humphrey began, "Okay, I'll have the Reuben combination with the curly fries, Caesar salad and a Diet Coke."

*Diet Coke?* Sandy thought. She hated Diet Coke. She hated anything diet—that NutraSweet taste was so nasty to her.

But she wasn't about to let her pastor think she was an independent, nonconforming, non-preacher's-wife-material kind of girl. So she just nodded in agreement and smiled as the waitress took her menu.

"You know," the pastor began, "you really didn't have to order what I ordered. Lunch is on me, and you're free to choose whatever you like on the menu."

"That's okay, Pastor." Sandy rubbed the palm of his hand. "Whatever you order is just fine. I believe you made the best choice for me."

Pastor Humphrey then smiled and shook his head.

Suddenly he jumped in his seat and almost knocked the table over when a woman in a red dress walked by.

"What's wrong?" Sandy asked.

"Did you see that?" Pastor Humphrey asked while looking behind him where the woman had seemingly disappeared into the crowd of other lunchtime patrons.

"Did I see what?" Sandy asked, not sure what he was talking about.

"That? Did you see her eyes? They were flashing red. Almost demonlike!"

Sandy didn't remember seeing the woman's eyes or noticing anything special about them. They looked pretty brown to her. "No, I didn't. I must have missed that."

"You *had* to have seen it," the pastor insisted, then nervously began to search the entire restaurant.

Sandy noticed that his forehead was dripping with sweat. He grabbed a napkin from the table to wipe it off.

"I'm sorry," the pastor said. "I think I'm having visions again."

"Visions?" Sandy asked with a concerned look. "What visions?"

"Visions of demons. I used to see evil spirits in people almost every day. They went away once I started my church two years ago, but lately they've been coming back.

"I know this may sound strange," Pastor Humphrey continued, "but before I started my church, I used to think the devil had a hit out on me!"

"A hit out on you?" Sandy asked curiously.

"Yes. A hit! All kinds of crazy stuff was happening to me. And sometimes I would walk out of my house and feel like I was being attacked by demons, so half the time I would be fighting them off me!" Pastor Humphrey violently waved both his hands in the air.

People from neighboring tables looked over at their table and whispered to each other.

"Oh, really," Sandy said.

"Then I prayed and asked God to take the visions away. I figured if I started a church, they would leave."

Sandy wasn't quite understanding. "So you started a church so demons wouldn't attack you?"

"Basically, yes. My goal is to kill the devil and his evil cohorts, so what better way to do that than to start a church! Even the Bible says that God will build His rock upon the church and that the gates of hell shall not prevail. So I'm ready, devil! I say, bring it on!"

Sandy was really bewildered at this point. She thought people started churches because they wanted to help people and save souls.

The waitress brought the identical meals and placed them on the table. Pastor Humphrey asked for a straw and Sandy did, as well.

Pastor Humphrey sipped his Diet Coke, and Sandy just looked at hers.

*Yuck,* she thought.

Once he finished his meal in less than ten minutes, Pastor Humphrey suggested he and his date make their way over to the museum next door.

Entering the museum floor arm in arm after having forgiven the pastor for his previous comments in the restaurant, Sandy was looking forward to eyeing art with her new boo—her new pastor boo, that is.

The two of them stopped to look at an original piece by a popular Detroit artist.

"I really like his work, don't you?" Pastor Humphrey asked Sandy.

"Uh-huh," she replied while not looking at the art but at her new male friend. Besides the acne on his forehead and razor bumps on his neck, she liked how his skin looked so smooth and how his sideburns were lined perfectly.

The two of them strolled to a standing statue of a half-naked man with only a piece of cloth wrapped around his waist.

Pastor Humphrey looked the statue up and down, then suddenly jumped backward.

"What is it?" Sandy asked.

*Not again,* Sandy thought.

"Oh, nothing," he said.

Not wanting to believe her date was crazy, Sandy decided it was time for her to take a little stroll of her own.

"Pastor Humphrey," Sandy began, "I'm a little thirsty. I think I'm going to mosey over here and get a drink at the water fountain next to the restroom."

"Want me to go with you?" the pastor asked.

"No, I'm okay," Sandy said as she slid out of the pastor's arm and made her way to the fountain.

As she took a long sip of water, then wiped her mouth with the back of her hand and reapplied her lip gloss using her makeup compact's mirror, Sandy didn't know what to think of her so-called date. He was acting really weird.

Sure, she had heard of evil spirits before, but never like this. Maybe she wasn't spiritual enough to see the spirits in the statues, she thought. Or maybe she just wasn't spiritual enough, period.

Sandy was making her way back toward Mr. Humphrey when she noticed him staring intently at a large colorful painting with many shapes such as circles and triangles on it. She could tell that he was talking to it from the way his mouth moved and the way he pointed at it like he was scolding it.

As she got closer, she could comprehend what he was saying, as he yelled, "Come out! Come out in the name of Jesus!" at the painting.

The closer she got to him, the louder he became.

The only couple who were in the museum with them looked at him strangely, clutched each other and made their way to the exit door.

"Come out, I say, you evil spirit, you! Legion? Come out!"

Suddenly Sandy became paralyzed where she stood.

Only a few feet away from him, she couldn't move any more.

She just stood and watched this man make a plum fool of himself.

She had had enough of this foolishness and immediately turned around and started running.

She ran so fast one of her heels came off as she made it to the exit door. She put it back on and made it through the door and started running down the block.

She stopped at a nearby bus stop and keeled over in order to catch her breath.

It was then that she realized she had no transportation

home. She thought about catching the bus, but with her lack of direction skills, she wasn't quite sure which route to take in order to make it to her destination.

She reached inside her purse and noticed that she had taken that wad of money that normally lay on her dresser at home.

"Thank you, Jesus!" she rang out loud, still breathing out of control.

She grabbed her cell and called a cab.

After a half hour a yellow cab pulled up to the corner where Sandy stood, and she immediately hopped inside.

"Where to, lady?" the Latino cabdriver wearing a black leather cap asked Sandy from the front as the glass separated the two of them.

"Twelve twenty-eight Forrer," Sandy replied as she tried to get comfortable in the smelly cab with torn vinyl seats.

Sandy was so befuddled she didn't even know how far she was away from home or how much it would even cost for her to get there. She didn't care, though. At that point all she wanted to do was go home.

The cabdriver turned left, drove down the street, then sat at a red light. Sandy looked to the right and spotted a certain royal-blue pickup truck that looked all too familiar. She glanced at the Michigan license plate, which read ACTS1N8.

It was Matthew's truck.

Just then Sandy spotted Matthew getting out of his truck with a bouquet of flowers in one hand and two brown grocery bags in the other.

He made his way up the porch steps of a brick two-floor

apartment building, where a brown-skinned girl with extremely long zillions and a protruding belly greeted him with open arms.

Sandy saw him set his grocery bags down and give the young woman a hug as the cabdriver turned the corner.

Sandy couldn't believe what she'd just witnessed. Liz's minister boyfriend, the most faithful man Sandy had ever known, out cheating on Liz with some young, pregnant chick? Giving her flowers and groceries?

*Was she carrying his baby?* Sandy thought. The nerve of him!

*Men are just dogs!* she concluded at that very moment as she violently dialed Liz's number on her cell.

"Hello," Liz answered.

"Liz?" Sandy asked, knowing it was her.

Liz thought it strange that Sandy was phoning her; they barely talked to each other on the phone.

"Yes. Oh, hey, Sandy. What's up, girl?"

"Uh, nothing, I guess." Sandy wasn't sure how to say it and started to think that maybe she'd made a mistake by calling her. How would she take it?

"C'mon, girl, quit playing." Liz chuckled. "What's up?"

"Uh…" Sandy hesitated.

"Spit it out!" Liz demanded. She didn't have time to play games. She was getting ready to throw down in the kitchen.

"Liz, uh, I just saw Matthew go up in some woman's apartment after giving her some flowers and a big, uh, nonchurch hug."

"What woman?" Liz demanded as the carton of eggs she'd grabbed from the fridge crashed on the floor.

"I don't know," Sandy continued. "Some brown-skinned chick with long braids."

The other end was silent.

"Hello?" Sandy asked.

"Where was the apartment?" Liz demanded.

Sandy had to think about that one for a moment. "On the corner of Sutherland and 6 Mile," she replied.

"Thanks. 'Bye," Liz said and hung up the phone.

Sandy wondered why Liz had abruptly gotten off the phone. She didn't want to hear the rest of her story? Maybe she didn't want to believe it was true, Sandy thought.

Sandy closed her flip cell phone and pondered about her recent string of bad luck with men.

At that moment her cell phone rang and she was almost scared to look at it to see who was calling.

She finally looked at it and saw a local number she didn't recognize. *Who could this be?*

Sandy answered just before it went to voice mail.

"Hello," she answered in a soft voice.

"Hi, Sandy?" asked an unfamiliar male voice.

"Yes?" Sandy said, still wondering who it was on the other end who knew her name and number.

"This is Pierre."

*Pierre,* Sandy thought. *What in the world is he doing calling me? How did he get my number?* Then again, she did remember Michelle calling her from Pierre's phone before. Maybe he'd kept the number in his phone.

"Oh, hi, Pierre," Sandy said, sounding as if she was used to receiving calls from him all the time.

"Hi. Are you busy?"

*Am I busy? Yes, busy sulking about sorry men…and you're another one of them, buddy!* Sandy thought.

Then again, she remembered Michelle telling her about how great a catch Pierre was, but for some reason Michelle no longer wanted to be with him. Something about God telling her to let him go.

However, Sandy couldn't understand why God would tell her to let Pierre Dupree go. At least he didn't cheat on her. And at least he wasn't gay.

"Uh, no, I'm not busy," Sandy said as she continued to gaze out the window during the seemingly never-ending cab ride.

"Good. Mind if I hook up with you tonight?"

"Hook up with me?" Sandy asked out loud.

"Yes. I just need to talk."

Sandy thought about his request as the cabdriver pulled in front of Madear's house.

She wouldn't mind going out with someone who was sane, especially after today's disastrous lunch date.

*The night is still young, and all Pierre wants to do is just talk to someone. Besides, Michelle wouldn't talk to him—and she wouldn't mind if I just talked to him as a friend, now, would she? Besides, she shouldn't mind,* Sandy concluded. *Michelle has two men chasing after her, and what do I have? Nothing. If Michelle doesn't want him, then she shouldn't mind me going out with Pierre just to talk. Especially since Michelle has made it plain and clear to Liz and I that she no longer wants anything to do with the brotha.*

"Um. Sure, we can talk," Sandy concluded.

However, she figured Madear wouldn't dare go for having Pierre over at her house. Madear had met Pierre before when Michelle and Pierre were an item, and Sandy didn't feel like having to explain herself to her grandmother.

"But," Sandy continued, "we can't talk at my house. We're going to have to meet somewhere."

"No problem," Pierre said. "I can pick you up. You feel like ice cream?"

"Ice cream sounds good," Sandy responded.

"Let's go out for some ice cream. Pick you up at eight?"

Sandy started thinking about her favorite cookies-and-cream ice cream and how good it would taste and how sweet it would be sitting across the booth from a man as fine as Mr. Pierre Dupree.

She felt as if she deserved a sweet treat, especially after all she'd been through lately with men.

"Eight is fine," she said and hung up the phone, paid the cabdriver and headed inside in order to prepare for her date—or night out with a friend, as she tried to convince herself.

# Chapter 19

*Slow Down*

Liz put her pedal to the metal and was doing eighty on the Southfield Freeway as she was on her way to the apartment building where Sandy said she'd spotted Matthew.

She was just about to exit onto McNichols when she noticed a white cop car follow her off the exit ramp.

As soon as she was stopped at a red light, she looked in the rearview mirror. When the light turned green, as she continued on, the cop flashed his lights on her.

The police car's siren went off and Liz pulled her car over to the nearby gas station.

"Oh, shoot!" Liz proclaimed as she scrambled around looking for her driver's license, car registration and proof of insurance.

She finally found her registration and proof of insurance

inside her glove box and was going through her wallet in her purse when the policeman tapped her window.

She rolled down the window and asked, "Is there a problem, Officer?"

"Is there a problem? You were going eighty on the freeway, then crossed lanes abruptly in order to exit 6 Mile," the tall, Caucasian policeman stated.

"I'm sorry, Officer, you're right. I was speeding. Please forgive me. I normally don't speed like that. I'm in the middle of an emergency situation," Liz said.

"What's the emergency?" the policeman asked.

Liz hadn't expected him to ask her that.

"My boyfriend may be cheating on me," Liz said in a low tone.

"What was that?" the policeman asked.

"I said my boyfriend may be cheating on me!" Liz responded louder than she'd wanted to. She was really upset and hoped the policeman didn't take her for some kind of crazy woman.

"Oh, I see," he said. "Ma'am, I'm going to need to see your license, registration and proof of insurance."

Liz obliged and gave the policeman everything he needed, and he went back to his police car to run her plates. Liz sat silently in her car, quietly praying for favor and that this cop will have mercy on her.

*Maybe I shouldn't have said the part about my boyfriend,* she thought.

After several minutes, the policeman returned to the car with a pink slip of paper. "I gave you a ticket for being ten miles over, even though you were really going twenty-five miles over the posted fifty-five miles-per-hour speed limit. Because you have a clean driving record, for the most part, I went ahead and gave you a break."

"Thank you, Officer," Liz said and took her ticket and stuffed it in her purse.

The officer continued, "Now, do you need me to escort you over to your boyfriend's house, because I don't want to have to get a call about you later tonight for something else."

Liz smiled slightly. "No, Officer. I'll be okay. I'll drive slower and I'll be fine."

"You sure will. Don't worry about it, okay? And try to have a nice day."

"Thanks," Liz said, rolled her window back up and sat in the car for a minute before driving off.

*Maybe this ticket was God's way of telling me it's not a good idea for me to try and catch Matthew with another woman,* she thought. *Maybe I should just call him.*

Liz dialed Matthew's phone number, and it rang six times, then went to voice mail.

Liz grew upset all over again. She knew her name and picture showed up on his cell anytime she called, yet he was still refusing to answer.

She pulled out of the gas station and headed toward the two-floor apartment building on the corner of 6 Mile and Sutherland, driving much more slowly this time.

# Chapter 20

*Sweet Treats*

The ice cream shop was surprisingly empty. Pierre and Sandy were the only two people seated inside the whole shop. Sandy thought that was actually romantic. It was as if Pierre had reserved the entire shop just for the two of them.

"Sandy, I just want to tell you that you look absolutely gorgeous," Pierre began as he played with his banana split while gazing into Sandy's blue eyes.

Sandy blushed. "Thanks," she replied.

"You know, I always thought you were gorgeous. Even more beautiful than Michelle—but, of course, I couldn't tell you that because, you know, I was with Michelle at the time."

"Uh-huh," Sandy said as she swirled her spoon around her bowl of two scoops of cookies-and-cream ice cream topped with whipped cream, nuts and a cherry.

"But now that me and Michelle have broken up, I feel more free to express my true feelings with you, Sandra A. Moore."

Sandy liked the way Pierre said her full name. His baritone voice and hazel eyes that were all on her sent chills up and down her spine.

"What's your middle name, Sandra?" he asked.

"My middle name?" Sandy asked with a smirk.

"Yeah. Your middle name."

"No one has ever asked me that before."

"Well I'm asking you," Pierre said.

"Well, okay, then. It's Anitra," Sandy said.

"A-ni-tra," Pierre repeated, over enunciating every syllable, which made Sandy blush. "I like that," he said. "Sandy," Pierre said and grabbed her free hand. "I've had my eye on you for quite some time now."

"Oh, really?" Sandy inquired with a suspicious tone.

"Really," Pierre said. He began to play with her fingers. "You're so vibrant and alive. I love your personality! Michelle was so boring and fussy all the time. But you, on the other hand, you're a woman I know would be good for me."

"How do you know this, Pierre?" Sandy asked.

"I know because I know," Pierre said in a sexy tone.

Sandy ate a spoonful of ice cream, licked the back of her spoon, then glared at him intensely.

Just sitting and talking with him was stirring up all types of sensations inside of her that she had initially suppressed.

"And I know what I want," Pierre stated, and with that he added, "Here, you have something on your cute little nose," then proceeded to wipe a speckle of whipped cream off her nose.

He then licked his finger that had the whipped cream on it.

Sandy giggled lightly and Pierre chuckled in return.

Next thing you know, Sandy gave a hearty laugh out loud and Pierre still chuckled and asked, "What's so funny?"

"Oh, nothing," Sandy said and then rested her hand underneath her chin. "Nothing at all, Pierre. It just feels good to laugh again."

"Okay. Well, that's good, then. You know the Word says a merry heart doeth good like a medicine."

"It sure does," Sandy agreed with a smile.

"I have joy right now, being here with you," Pierre said in all seriousness.

"You make me happy, too, Pierre," Sandy replied.

"I'm glad," he said, then added, "You know, I still need to get some things off my chest, but, to be honest, I don't feel comfortable telling all of my business in this public setting."

Sandy looked around and only saw the lone ice cream scooper behind the counter, staring at the two of them.

Pierre continued, "Mind if we go back to my place so I can be more open and honest and real?"

Sandy thought about his request. *Should I go back to his place? What would Michelle think? Would she approve of it?* Sandy thought that maybe going back to his place wouldn't be such a good idea.

*But Michelle's not interested in Pierre anymore,* Sandy remembered, even though she couldn't tell why in the world she wasn't interested in him. *Well, if she doesn't want him,* Sandy concluded, *then there's no reason a good man should go to waste. He's a good catch for somebody, and that somebody just might be me. Maybe.*

# Chapter 21

*Night Patrol*

Liz slowly drove and crept up to the apartment complex she was looking for. Sure enough, there was Matthew's blue pickup truck with the ACTS1N8 license plate on the back.

Liz thought about walking up to the apartment complex but decided against it because she didn't know the woman's name nor her apartment number.

Liz parked her black Sebring in the alley, kitty-corner to the complex so she could still get a good view of the front of the complex while remaining out of view when Matthew walked out—so she could catch him red-handed.

After sitting for an hour, Liz grabbed her prepared lunch from her lunch bag and started munching on a ham-and-cheese sandwich and some macaroni and cheese and green beans she'd packed in Tupperware containers. She sipped on her fruit punch in a thermos and noticed the truck still sitting there.

After she was done eating, she grabbed her Bible and opened it in an attempt to allow God to order her steps as she turned the pages.

She found herself at 2 Samuel and began reading about David and Bathsheba, then got mad all over again and closed the book and just looked out the window.

She noticed a young couple leaving their car parked in front of the complex and begin walking up to the main entrance.

Liz hopped out of her car in the alley, then made her way to the couple and asked, "Excuse me, do you live in this complex?"

The couple looked at each other, then the man replied, "Yes."

"Oh, good," Liz said. "Have you noticed this blue truck here a lot?" The couple looked at each other again and this time the woman responded. "Well, yes, I've seen it here a few times."

Liz grew even more upset and felt like keying Matthew's car right then and there.

She continued talking to the two strangers. "Have you seen the gentleman who owns this car and, if so, do you know the room number that he goes to when he's here?"

The man, apparently now agitated, said, "Well, no, but if we did know, we sure wouldn't tell you!" And with that, he grabbed on to his girlfriend's arm and the two of them made it inside their apartment complex.

"Well, that didn't work," Liz said, then headed back to her car parked in the alley.

She laid her seat back, fell asleep and woke up at around eleven o'clock.

She looked in front of the apartment complex.

The truck was still there.

Liz was heartbroken and sobbed quietly in her car.

She couldn't believe Matthew was cheating on her and staying over some woman from his church's place well into the night.

Defeated, hungry, thirsty and now having to go to the bathroom, Liz turned the ignition key in her car and decided to drive home. She looked at her cell phone once more to see if Matthew had ever returned her call.

He hadn't.

# Chapter 22

*A Hurting Heart*

Sandy entered Pierre's condominium downtown and immediately admired its modern black-and-silver decor.

The front room was like an art gallery, with different African-American art and the famous piece of the man's black biceps with his hands in shackles and chains and the photo of the two black sculptures of a man and a woman's bodies intertwined with one another.

Sandy's heels clicked loudly as she walked across the waxed hardwood floor as Pierre proceeded to give her a tour of his place.

With each picture he showed her, he turned on its own light, which hung directly above each one.

"This one here is one of my favorites," Pierre told Sandy as they stood in front of a picture of an African-American woman with her hair wrapped like a Muslim, with tears running down her face.

"Why is she crying?" Sandy asked, holding on to Pierre's arm.

"It's a picture of a black Mary," Pierre answered. "She's crying as she is about to witness Jesus, her Son, about to be hanged on the cross."

"It's beautiful," Sandy beamed as she stared intently at the portrait.

"Kinda makes you sad, doesn't it?" Pierre asked Sandy while staring at her.

Sandy returned the glance. "Yes, it does." Sandy couldn't get over how sexy Pierre looked tonight. She felt like unbuttoning the rest of the buttons on his gray silk shirt. Instead she took her hand and placed it on his chest, rested her head on his shoulder and sneaked a whiff of his sweet-smelling cologne.

"I know," Pierre said, back to looking at the picture. "It kinda reminds me of how I felt when Michelle took her love away from me," Pierre stated with lowered eyes.

Sandy looked at Pierre with compassion and gave his chest a light squeeze. "I'm so sorry, Pierre."

"That's okay," he said and grabbed her hand, which held on to his chest. "I'll get over it. Life goes on, right?" Pierre added, then broke away from Sandy's embrace and made his way over to the front room, grabbed the remote and turned his movie-screen TV on the jazz music station.

He sat on his long black leather couch and just stared at the screen, bobbing his head with the music.

Sandy went over and sat next to Pierre, placing her hand on his thigh.

"Pierre," she said.

He ignored her and kept bobbing his head.

"Pierre," Sandy repeated, noticing that she still couldn't get his attention. "I know what Michelle did to you was wrong and I'm sorry that happened to you. But you can't beat yourself up for it."

Pierre remained stoic.

Sandy continued, "You can't just sit here and sulk."

He finally turned toward Sandy. "Do you know all I've done for that woman? I asked her to marry me, for God's sake, and she practically slammed the door in my face! Do you know how that hurts?" he asked Sandy with an angry look on his face. "I forgot—you *don't* know. I pray you never experience the pain that I went through…or that I'm going through right now."

Sandy felt as though she could feel his pain.

She felt as if she could feel his anger and his suffering. She could sense he was hurt badly and she didn't like to see him this way. She liked seeing him smiling and laughing. She wanted the old, confident Pierre Dupree back. The world needed to have him back.

"Pierre," Sandy continued, "don't be like that. I mean, I understand you're hurting and all, but you have to get over it. You have to realize that there's a whole world out there and that there's a line of women out here who would love to call you their man."

After a brief pause Pierre looked over at Sandy. "Are you one of them?" he asked.

Sandy returned the glance. Though she didn't want to admit it, she had liked Pierre all along. She was intrigued by him and she believed that he was all the man Michelle said he was. She couldn't understand why Michelle decided to let him go.

"Yes," she finally admitted.

Pierre then leaned over to kiss Sandy, and she didn't resist.

He kissed her slowly and lightly on her glossy pink lips, and when she returned his kiss, he grabbed her and kissed her more heavily.

He then pulled her tiny frame on top of him and they lay kissing and groping each other on the couch.

In the next moment, he arose, still kissing her, picked her up and carried her to his bedroom and rolled her onto his king-size waterbed.

He crawled on top of her, and the two of them continued kissing and holding one another and rolling around the bed.

He kissed her on her neck and Sandy moaned with delight.

It'd been a while since she'd felt a man's body on top of her. She didn't want him to stop.

However, a still, small voice in the back of her mind whispered, *Sandy, no*. She shook off that voice and continued to French-kiss Pierre.

When Pierre slipped his hand underneath Sandy's dress and slid her pink lace panties down, Sandy suddenly had a flashback of her episode with Carter. While still kissing, Sandy moaned, "No, baby" and slowly pulled her panties back up.

"Trust me," Pierre said and rubbed his hands back up her thighs again to reach for her unmentionables once more. "I won't get you pregnant," he assured her.

*Pregnant?* Sandy suddenly thought. *Oh, no, not that, I definitely don't want that!*

"No, baby," she whispered once more and this time Pierre obliged.

They continued to roll on the waterbed well into the night, kissing each other and holding each other until they both fell asleep.

# Chapter 23

*If Walls Could Talk*

"He's what?" Michelle asked Liz on her office phone at work Tuesday morning. Liz was at home cooking breakfast.

"Girl, he's cheating on me!" Liz said while banging her frying pan against the eye of her electric stove, as if that would make it get hotter even quicker.

"How do you know?" Michelle asked while chewing on a pencil and peeking out her window, making sure no one was looking at her.

"Well, his truck was parked outside this lady from his church's apartment practically all night!" Liz exclaimed.

"How do you know that?" Michelle asked.

"That's not important. The point is, Sandy told me she saw him give some girl some flowers and a big hug, and I went by where Sandy saw his truck and confirmed that she was telling the truth."

"So you were spying on him?" Michelle asked. She'd never thought her best friend would stoop to that level.

"I wasn't spying," Liz said. "I was just…seeking confirmation. And I got it."

"Well, what are you going to do now?"

"I don't know. I have to call him out on it, I guess. I tried calling him yesterday, but of course it went straight to voice mail. Girl, I can't believe this! I had no idea he would cheat on me!" Liz said and plopped four slices of bacon on the frying pan.

"But, Liz, did you actually see him with the woman?" Michelle asked, not fully convinced.

"Well, no."

"So you don't really know if he's cheating on you or not!"

"I *do* know. I know he was at that girl's house, and Sandy saw it, too!"

"C'mon, now, Liz. We're talking about Sandy here. You know that girl gets faces mixed up all the time. It probably wasn't even him."

"But I saw his truck!"

"All I'm saying is don't assume anything. You need to talk to him yourself. Don't write him off so soon."

"I don't know, girl."

"You know what?" Michelle said as she suddenly thought of a brilliant idea. "I think with my breakups from David and Pierre and your issues with Matthew that we deserve a little break from all this drama. Did you hear about that Christian party DJ L—S.O.S. is throwing this Saturday night?"

"No, I hadn't heard about it," Liz admitted.

"CJ is supposed to be there performing. We should go! We need to unwind and have some fun!"

"You're sure right about that," Liz said as she thought about whether or not she should attend. She hadn't been to a Christian party in over a year, and even though she was not a big fan of the heavy crowds and young faces, she enjoyed seeing her friends from church and the positive atmosphere—and, of course, the fried chicken wings with hot sauce they offer for only three dollars.

"Let's go!" Michelle decided for Liz. "As a matter of fact, let's have a sleepover at my place on Saturday, and we can all go to church together Sunday morning. Remember when we used to have those?"

"Yeah, about five years ago," Liz said.

"Well, let's have another one, this Saturday. I'll have popcorn and we can order pizza! I'll call Sandy," Michelle said as she made up her mind that she was going to host it.

"Sandy?" Liz asked. She'd thought this was going to be an opportunity for her and her best friend to hang out— just the two of them.

"Yeah, Sandy. It'll be a great way to expose her to some good, clean, Christian fun!"

"Okay, then," Liz gave in.

"Cool! I'll call Sandy. Oh, and meet at my place around five on Saturday."

"Okay," Liz found herself saying, then hung up the phone.

Even though she hadn't quite begun her workload for the day, Michelle figured she'd call Sandy now before she forgot.

Sandy opened her eyes Monday morning and barely recognized her surroundings. She looked at the silver desk with the desktop computer, the black-silver chair and the picture of Malcolm X on the wall, which, for some reason, looked fuzzy as she tried to make it out.

She tried to sit up but couldn't because the foreign bed she lay in kept moving around, causing her to lose balance.

She looked to her left and saw Pierre's back.

She rolled back over, lifted up the black satin comforter to look at her body and saw she had on only her pink lace bra and panties. She then lay on her back and stared at the ceiling. She looked on the floor to the left and spotted the rest of her clothes, then looked back up at the ceiling.

*Oh. My. God,* she thought. *What in the world did I just do? What would Michelle think? What would Madear think? What does God think?*

Sandy heard a loud snore come from Pierre as she looked back over at him. She couldn't believe she'd spent the night with him. *At least they didn't do it,* she thought to herself, but she may as well have since they still spent the night in the same bed.

Sandy suddenly grew nervous—and guilty.

She'd never spent the night with one of her girlfriend's ex-boyfriends before. Her girlfriends' boyfriends and exes would definitely hit on her, but she never gave in to their advances.

She tried to convince herself that Michelle didn't want Pierre anyway, but she still felt bad about everything. If Michelle walked in on the two of them right now, what in the world would she say?

Suddenly Sandy's cell phone rang.

Sandy reached over to the silver nightstand and grabbed her phone as she continued to lie in the bed. She saw that it was Michelle calling her. *Oh, no,* Sandy thought.

Sandy always answered Michelle's calls, so she knew if she didn't answer, then she might think something was wrong. Besides, it was Michelle who'd first sensed something was wrong when Carter had been about to rape her.

Sandy hoped that Michelle's divine instincts didn't intervene this time and somehow let her know that one of her best friends just spent the night with her ex.

"Hello," Sandy said in a low, raspy tone.

"Hey, Sandy, girl, how are you?" Michelle asked with a chipper voice, anxious to let Sandy know about her splendid idea.

"I'm fine," Sandy muttered.

"Oh, I'm sorry, did I wake you?"

"Yeah, kinda," Sandy said and looked over at the clock, which read ten o'clock.

"You're not working today?" Michelle asked.

"I close the store today, so I go in at one."

"Oh. Well, the reason I was calling was because I wanted to invite you to my place this Saturday so we can have a sleepover!"

"A sleepover?" Sandy asked while rubbing her eyes, then

she peeked over at Pierre to make sure he was still asleep. His back was still facing her.

"Yeah, a sleepover. Wouldn't that be fun? Oh, and there's also a party DJ L—S.O.S. is throwing that night, so we can all ride and go together!" Michelle said with a sip of her caramel latte.

"A party? Oh, well, okay. It sounds fun," Sandy said. She had never been to a Christian party before.

Just then Pierre let out another loud snore.

"Michelle, I gotta go. I'll talk to you later," Sandy said, then abruptly hung up the phone.

Michelle stared at the phone and thought to herself, *That was weird.*

Sandy stared at the wall as she thought about her friend. *Michelle is going to kill me,* she thought.

"Was that Michelle?" the deep, husky voice with its back facing Sandy grumbled.

"Yeah," Sandy replied, still spaced out looking at the wall.

"Mmm," Pierre replied. "Tell her I said go to hell."

Sandy closed her eyes tightly. She couldn't believe what Pierre just said. The hatred he felt for Michelle in his heart was too much for Sandy to bear. Sure, she may have been wrong for cutting him out of her life, but she was still one of her best friends.

Sandy crawled out of the waterbed and started to get dressed.

Pierre crawled over on his back, sat up and looked at her and said, "Where do you think you're going, young lady?"

"I have to go," Sandy said as she zipped up her dress. "This was all a big mistake."

"A mistake?" Pierre asked and sat up. "What do you mean by that?"

"I shouldn't be here. I shouldn't have spent the night last night. This was all wrong. I'm sorry, Pierre."

"Is that what you think? That this is all wrong?" he asked with a concerned look on his face.

"Yes," Sandy admitted.

"Oh, well, go on and think it, then. If you ask me, both of y'all crazy," he said and then rolled back over on his side and closed his eyes.

Sandy, fully clothed now, left his bedroom, grabbed her purse from the couch and slammed the door shut.

"What a punk!" Sandy cried.

Sandy waited a few moments to see if Pierre would come running out the door, following after her.

He didn't.

*He doesn't even care,* Sandy thought as she fiercely marched off while fighting back tears.

# Chapter 24

*Something to Shout About*

"So have you heard from David?" Liz asked from Michelle's love seat, eating popcorn while Michelle was seated on the floor in front of her brown couch, with Sandy seated on the couch. The three of them were at Michelle's apartment Saturday night, sitting in front of the TV, talking and watching gospel music videos.

"No," Michelle said while dipping a green apple slice in its caramel sauce. "Girl, I haven't heard from David or Pierre since last week. I'm sure they're both through with me right about now."

Sandy lowered her eyes. She then looked up and asked Michelle, "But isn't that what you wanted?"

"Yeah, I guess. More than anything I wanted to obey God. But it still gets hard sometimes. I miss them both."

Liz nodded her head and munched on another handful of popcorn.

"I mean," Michelle continued, "sometimes I wish I could take Pierre's charm, David's zeal for God, Pierre's looks, David's respect for women, Pierre's romantic side and David's singing talent...and mesh it all into one man. Now that would be ideal for me! That would be my perfect mate!"

"Yeah, that would—but nobody's perfect, Michelle," Liz reminded her friend.

"I know," Michelle agreed. "I guess I can't have it all."

"Michelle, now you know that's not true. You know that the man that God has for you is for you. Right now, as you obey God and pray about the whole situation, God will reveal to you what you should do and who you should be with," Liz said.

"You're right," said Michelle.

"Who do you want to be with?" Sandy asked out of her own curiosity.

"I want to be with them both!" Michelle shouted, then they all laughed.

"Well, you can't have your cake and eat it, too, Miss Thang!" Liz stated. "You gotta save something for the single women out here believing God for a mate! It's already seven women to one man, so you can't take two of 'em!"

All three ladies cracked up.

"I know, I know. I can't be stingy." Michelle added, "I just have to trust God and believe that I'm doing the right thing by giving it some time for me to pray and figure things out. I guess I'm secretly afraid I may lose the one that God has for me, if it's either one of them."

"Michelle Williamson, you and the word *lose* do not belong in the same sentence," Liz stated. "You're a woman of God, right?"

"Right," Michelle said sheepishly.

"So that means, since you obey God, you also have a covenant with God, so whatever He has promised you, which *includes* the mate of His choice, will come to pass in His season for your life."

"That's right," Michelle said, agreeing with Liz's words, which she had embedded in her mind but not quite yet in her heart.

"So don't worry about it!" Liz chimed.

"I know, girl. You're right," Michelle said.

Sandy interjected, "But I see where Mickey's coming from, Liz. Lately it's just been so hard to find a good man— or, I'm sorry, for us single Christian women to wait to be found by a good man. I mean, it's hard enough to find a man who is not locked up or on drugs. But to find a man who's saved, too? Now that's a tall order!"

"I know, girl. And today, being saved isn't enough," Liz chimed in. "You got so many people going around saying they're saved just because it's the, quote-unquote, 'in thing' to be right now. You gotta be careful out here."

"I know that's right," Michelle added. "He's saved...but does he have a personal relationship with God?"

"Or," Liz added, "he's saved...but is he living right?"

"Or, I got one," Sandy added. "He's saved...but is he straight?"

All three of them cracked up laughing.

"Or what about this one?" Liz added. "He's saved...but does he have a checking account?"

They all laughed again.

"He's saved," Michelle added, "but does he have bad credit?"

"Or he's saved," Sandy said, "but does he have a j-o-b?"

Michelle and Liz laughed and gave each other a high five.

"He's saved," Michelle added while looking dreamy-eyed toward the ceiling, "but is he sincere?"

"He's saved," Liz added while munching on another handful of popcorn, "but is he faithful?"

"He's saved," Sandy added, "but is he flat-out crazy?"

All three of them cracked up laughing again, with Michelle rolling on the floor.

"He's saved," Liz started again, "but is he holy?"

"He's saved," Sandy said, "but is he a deadbeat dad?"

"I know that's right, girl," Liz added. "What about this one? He's saved...but has he really tried Jesus?"

Liz started clapping as Sandy was keeled over shouting and praising God.

"You see, we gotta believe, my sisters!" Michelle said.

"Uh-huh," Liz said, imitating a preacher in a pulpit.

"We gotta believe in His Word! We gotta believe in His promises! We gotta believe in His love for us!" Michelle continued. "He knows the ending before the beginning! He's the Alpha and the Omega! He knows the final outcome! He *holds* the final outcome! You see, weeping may endure for a moment, but joy comes in the morning!"

Liz shot up and shouted, "Hallelujah!"

"Though it may not look like it on the outside…though statistics may not seem to be in our favor…we gotta believe that God is not a God of statistics, He is a God of making the impossible…*possible!*"

"Glory to God!" Liz shouted.

Michelle, Sandy and Liz then proceeded to have a praisefest right there in Michelle's front room, shouting, jumping and praising God and exuding great joy, unspeakable joy which was full of glory.

After twenty minutes of shouting and praising God, Michelle looked over at the clock and noticed that it was after nine o'clock.

"Well, ladies," Michelle said, out of breath, "we been so busy praising God we hadn't even noticed the time! The party started over an hour ago!"

Liz sat on the couch, out of breath from praising God herself, and asked, "You sure you still wanna go?"

"Yeah, I still wanna go!" Michelle said as a matter of fact. "CJ is one of my favorite contemporary gospel artists. Hopefully we haven't missed him!"

"Girl, you know we haven't missed him yet," Liz assured her. "He's probably going to be one of the last acts of the party!"

"Well, I better get dressed now so I can look good for all of my fans," Sandy said, moseying her little hips over to the bathroom before anyone else could get in before her. "'Cause tonight," she added self-assuredly, "I'm believing God for favor with God and a man!"

Liz rolled her eyes. "You mean favor with God and man, you silly girl."

"That, too," Sandy said with a smile and shut the bathroom door.

# Chapter 25

*Party Over Here!*

Sandy, Liz and Michelle walked into the small fellowship hall and each paid their ten-dollar entry fee.

Inside the party Sandy looked around in awe. The dimness and flashing lights from the disco ball in the center of the dance floor gave the church's fellowship hall a clublike feel to it. A cluster of women covered the dance floor as they ballroom hustled to Kierra KiKi Sheard's "Why Me?"

Sandy looked around the hall and noticed that there was a significantly larger number of women than men, but she wasn't surprised. The few men she did see looked even younger than she was, but they were kinda cute.

"C'mon, let's hustle," Michelle said and grabbed Sandy by the arm, this time leading her onto the dance floor.

"Okay," Sandy said and looked over at Liz for her to join them.

"Y'all girls go on and enjoy yourselves," Liz said. "Y'all know I'm not one into all this dancing and going on. I'll be over here," Liz said and pointed toward the kitchen.

"Okay, then, suit yourself!" Sandy shouted as Liz walked away, then Sandy joined right in with the group of women hustling. She made sure she was in front of everyone else, in case she caught the eye of a cute hottie.

"What's up, y'all? This is DJ L—S.O.S. coming to you live in the D, and that's DJ Lord Save our Sooouuuls train!" the DJ shouted, then laughed in the microphone from the stage up front. "I just want to thank y'all for coming out tonight so we can all party and have fun in Jesus' Name!" he said and took a swig from his bottled water. "I see the ladies got the hustle going on over there on the dance floor. Hey, Michelle, I see you, girl!"

Michelle looked up at DJ L—S.O.S. at the DJ booth and gave him a smile and a wave to acknowledge his shout-out, then continued to hustle.

Michelle suddenly spotted David entering the party.

He gave the guys dap and the ladies hugs as he made his way closer to the dance floor.

Michelle's heart dropped as she noticed how cute he looked tonight. He was faded up with a goatee and had on some nice jeans and a blue-and-white-striped collared shirt. Michelle liked this new preppy look on him. Even though she had gone with him over a year before she recently broke up with him, for some reason he looked cuter tonight than she had ever seen him.

Once the song was over, the hustlers dispersed and left Michelle and Sandy on the dance floor, wondering what song was going to come on next.

Next thing you know, a large group of people entered the floor and started waving their hands and moving from side to side as DJ L—S.O.S. played a favorite contemporary gospel jam, "Temptation" by J.R.

Sandy grew excited as all of the people flooded the dance floor around the two of them. Even though she had never heard the song before, she loved the beat and began doing a little moving on her own as the song declared, *"Lord Jesus will you keep my mind, 'cause I'm weak in the flesh, I'm about to wild out!"*

Sandy threw her hands in the air, waved them from side to side, then stuck her behind out and started moving from side to side with the music. She then stood up straight and starting doing a pop dance, thrusting her practically nonexistent chest.

The few guys who were in the party started looking at Sandy, who was getting her dance on while winking at her admirers.

Michelle eventually grabbed Sandy's arm and led her off the dance floor as if she were her parent.

"Girl, what in the world are you doing?" Michelle said to Sandy off to the side, away from the party crowd.

"What? I was just having a little fun," Sandy said with a sly smirk.

"Well, this is a Christian party, so I suggest you leave all that booty shakin' at the club!" Michelle sternly told her.

"Ugh, Michelle, you're starting to sound like Liz," Sandy said to her friend.

"Where is Liz, anyway?" Michelle asked, then looked around the hall for her.

"Probably somewhere near the food," Sandy said. Sure enough, the two of them spotted Liz standing by the kitchen with a chicken wing in one hand and a cup of red pop in the other.

She was laughing and talking to David.

"There she is," Sandy said, pointing in her direction.

"Don't point. That's rude," Michelle said, wondering if she should go over there now since Liz was chatting with her ex.

Before Michelle could give it another thought, Sandy grabbed Michelle's arm and said, "C'mon, let's go over there."

"Hey, y'all," Liz said with a mouth smeared with fried chicken grease. "Look who I ran into—good ole David!"

David looked over at Sandy, then locked his eyes on Michelle.

"Hi, David!" Sandy sang, then gave him a hug.

"Hey, Miss Sandy!" David returned her exuberance. "Hey, Michelle," David said in a monotone voice, staring at her.

"Hey, David," Michelle said while not making a single move toward hugging him.

"David here has a wonderful testimony to share! Go on, tell 'em," Liz said while licking her fingers.

"Oh, well, it's nothing really."

"Nothing?" Liz exclaimed. "Oh, yes, it *is* something! It's something big! If you don't tell 'em, then I will…."

"I'll tell 'em," David said, then again locked eyes with Michelle. "I'm being sent to be the praise team leader of our sister church in Atlanta."

"Well, glory to God!" Michelle said calmly with a smile.

"And tell them the rest," Liz egged him on.

"What rest?" David asked, not quite sure.

"About you being on staff there and everything."

"Oh, well, it's not exactly 'on staff.' Basically I'll be getting a salary as the praise team leader."

"A salary?" Sandy said in a chipper tone.

"So that means you'll be getting paid to sing?" Michelle said.

"Yeah," David said, still looking at Michelle.

"David, that's been your dream! Praise the Lord!" Michelle jumped up and down and gave David a big hug. He returned her embrace and closed his eyes as she kept holding him tight.

Sandy and Liz eyed each other suspiciously, then looked back at David and Michelle, who were still embracing.

Eventually Michelle let go and regained her composure by smoothing out her denim dress and combing her hair with her fingers, embarrassed about her outward show of emotion.

"Excuse me," Michelle said. "I'm just so happy for you, David!"

"That's okay," David said, then looked at her. "You always were very supportive of anything I did, and I know you're happy for me."

Michelle looked on the ground as an uneasy silence filled the air.

"So when do you leave?" Sandy asked excitedly.

"Oh, in about a month," David said.

"A month?" Michelle asked. She hadn't known it would be that soon.

"Yeah. I was happy to get that much notice. Most of the time when you get sent to a sister church, you might get only two weeks' notice."

"Oh," Michelle said in a lowered tone.

"Why, Michelle? Are you sad to see me go?" David asked.

"No." Michelle perked up. "I'm happy you're leaving. I mean, it's your dream come true—a full-time singer," she said with a smile.

David smiled at her in return.

"All right, y'all!" DJ L—S.O.S. yelled in the microphone. "I want y'all to get ready for the one y'all really came to see! The one, the only, *Mr. Canton Jones!*"

Screams and cheers were heard all over the place as CJ made his way to the stage with his music playing in the background. The crowd started dancing wildly, bouncing up and down as "Everybody Dancing" played in the background and CJ sang the chorus.

Sandy and Michelle jumped up and down to the beat in the front of the crowd, too, while Liz sat down at a nearby table and nodded her head.

Liz suddenly wondered what Matthew was doing right about now, especially since she hadn't heard from him today or last night.

She arose and slipped to the door outside the women's restroom and gave him a call.

After about four rings, a young female's voice answered Matthew's phone. "Hello?"

"Aw, hex naw!" Liz said and immediately shut her flip cell phone and decided right then that it was time for her to confront her man about this other woman—once and for all.

Liz dashed out the front door without even saying goodbye to her friends, who were still in the crowd, having a Holy Ghost good time singing right along with CJ.

CJ sang about six of his songs, then he switched up the pace and began to sing and worship God. Everyone in the audience lifted their hands in order to praise and worship God as His sweet Spirit began to fill the room.

Young people keeled over, prayed in tongues and worshipped God. Some young men lay prostrate on the floor as God's presence filled the place.

Michelle felt every burden be lifted from her shoulders as she lifted her hands high and opened them wide and received all the love that He has for her. She started crying and thinking about His goodness and His magnificence and His awesomeness.

Sandy was crying, as well. She had her arms wrapped around herself and was quietly sobbing.

"Glory to God, hallelujah!" DJ L—S.O.S. yelled into the mic as the crowd praised God right along with him. "Now that's what I'm talking about! God is good!"

"All the time," the crowd of zealous partygoers responded.

"Y'all know what?" DJ L—S.O.S. said. "I still feel that the

Lord's not done. If there is anyone here who, for whatever reason, has missed it in any way and you feel like you've sinned and fallen away from God and need to be brought back in fellowship with Him, please come up front." He panned the crowd and no one responded.

"If you feel like you missed it or failed God or feel like you need restoration in your life, know that it's a new day, and today can be a day of new beginnings for you. God's mercies are great and His compassions fail not. Receive His grace and mercy on today." DJ L—S.O.S. searched the room and still no one came forward.

Michelle stood still with her eyes closed and her hands locked in front of her face in a prayer position, as she prayed quietly in tongues to herself. She eventually opened her eyes and saw Sandy beside her, keeled over, crying hysterically, with a runny nose.

Sandy's sobbing grew louder and louder as Michelle looked around for Liz for additional support, who was nowhere to be found.

Michelle rubbed Sandy's back, then Sandy let out a scream and started bawling like a baby. Michelle knelt beside Sandy and quietly asked her, "Do you want to go down to the front?"

Sandy nodded her head wildly while still refusing to move, so Michelle grabbed Sandy's hand and led her down as the crowd cheered them on.

Michelle thought it weird that Sandy would even need to go down to receive rededication. Michelle hadn't known Sandy's relationship with God had slipped. She again looked around for Liz and still couldn't spot her best friend anywhere.

"Glory to God! You're the one we've been waiting for!" DJ L—S.O.S. assured Sandy as she made her way to the front of the stage. Sandy's tear-drenched face faced the floor.

"You know the Word of God says if we confess our faults one to another, we shall be healed. So receive your healing today, woman of God!" Sandy looked up at the DJ as if he were a foreign creature, then she looked around as if she didn't recognize her surroundings. Everything looked blurry, and she felt as if she was in the twilight zone.

Sandy then looked at her friend next to her, who was holding her hand and lovingly rubbing her back in a slow, circular motion.

"Michelle," Sandy said so only Michelle could hear her.

"Yes, Sandy," Michelle replied with a warm smile.

"I slept with Pierre last night."

"You did *what!*" Michelle shouted and immediately let go of Sandy's hand.

# Chapter 26

*Busted*

Liz was doing eighty-five on the Lodge Freeway as she was on her way to take care of Minister Matthew Long once and for all. She was tired of the lies, tired of his cheating and tired of his wicked ways.

No longer was she going to stand for being second place in this relationship. No longer was she going to resort to being the one who got thrown into voice mail every time she called or the one who was known as the irrational one or the one who was "overreacting." That woman answering his cell phone—the one she bought him for Christmas last year—was enough reason for her to finally give this supposed man of the cloth a piece of her sanctified mind.

Liz pulled in front of the apartment building and, sure

enough, once again she spotted Matthew's blue truck parked out front.

Now Liz needed to figure out how to catch him red-handed even though she didn't know the other woman's name or apartment number.

Liz parked in her same spot in the alley and began the waiting game.

After twenty minutes of waiting with no success, Liz thought of an idea.

She called Matthew's phone again, and this time he answered after the fourth ring.

"Hello?"

"Hey, Matthew, sweetie, how are you?" Liz said in the sweetest voice she could muster.

"I'm fine, Liz. What's up?"

"Actually, a lot is up. I'm actually in an emergency situation right now with Mom and I really need your help."

"What's wrong? Is everything okay?"

"Well, no, it's not. I prefer not to explain over the phone, but if you could make it over here as soon as possible, I can explain everything once we get on our way to the hospital."

"The hospital? What's wrong with Ms.——"

"I can't say. Can you just make it over here? Fast?"

"Sure! I'm on the way!" Matthew said, then hung up the phone.

Liz closed her cell and smiled as she got out of the car and headed toward the front of the complex.

Five minutes later Matthew stormed out of the complex, with the other woman standing at the door behind him.

He was about to rush to his truck when he turned around, went back to the door and gave the woman a hug and assured her, "I'll be back."

"I'm sure you will," Liz yelled from the sidewalk with her arms folded, eyeing the man she'd once loved and thought would be the father of her children.

"Liz!" Matthew said in shock. "You're here! I—I thought you needed me to come over your house? Is everything okay?"

"No, everything is *not* okay," Liz said as she sashayed her hips up the walkway of the complex. "It's *especially* not okay when I find my man here at this apartment complex with some other chick!"

"Liz, let me explain…."

"Oh, yeah, you need to explain, all right. You need to explain why your truck been at this apartment complex all hours of the night for several days and why you don't answer your phone!"

"Liz, you been spying on me?" Matthew asked.

"You need to explain why you *lied* to me, telling me you weren't going to call this heifer back that gave you her phone number in church, when in fact you did call her back and are seeing her on the side! I'm no side dish, Minister Matthew Long. You need to turn in your ordination card."

"But, Liz, I can't believe you—"

"You can't believe *me?*" Liz got in Matthew's face. "I can't believe *you!* And to think, I *almost* thought you were a good man. I *almost* thought you were a good father. I *almost* thought that you *really* loved the Lord. But it turns out you're nothing but a joke!"

Liz then looked the other woman up and down. "Hmph. You need to give your high-schooler girlfriend here some more money so she can get her hair done. Those braids been in a little too long, sweetie!"

The young girl then slammed the door in Liz's face, leaving the two of them on the porch alone.

"Don't go there, Liz," Matthew said in a saddened tone.

"Oh, I went there. Since *you* went there, I went there. And if I wasn't saved, I would tell you where else you should go. It's *over!*" Liz said and stormed off the porch and headed to her car.

"Liz!" Matthew yelled from the porch. Liz didn't respond but kept walking briskly, looking mean as ever.

"Liz!" Matthew yelled again at the top of his lungs, with no response. "She's my sister!"

Liz stopped dead in her tracks and froze like a statue.

# Chapter 27

*Left Behind*

"I spent the night at Pierre's the other night," Sandy told me again in a voice so low I could barely hear her. Or maybe I didn't want to hear her. She started crying even louder and grew even more hysterical, drawing even more attention to the two of us. I had hoped no one noticed the shocked look on my face. They *slept* together? This just had to be a joke. I didn't even know the two of them were talking. Last thing I knew, Pierre was trying to get back with me, and now he'd *slept* with Sandy?

I looked at the girl beside me, all hunched over, crying like a four-year-old who'd lost her new toy. Who knows whether her apology was sincere. Tears don't mean anything. She probably just felt guilty. Holy Ghost probably pressed her so much that she felt she had to do the right thing by telling the truth. But why here? Why now? What, am I supposed to forgive her just because she's at the altar? I thought she was supposed to be my good friend. Now this girl next to me, crying like something crazy, looks like a complete stranger. Who is this chick and how could she be so stupid?

My body grew numb. My feet were glued to the floor as I panned the crowd, noticing everyone's praying hands reaching out toward Sandy. Look at that, all the compassion and remorse for the dear, poor, remorseful soul. What about me? I'm the one who needs hands stretched toward. This tramp just slept with my man! Or ex-man—but it's still the same. He still was mine. Even if he wasn't, unspoken rule number one in friend circles is you don't go around messing with your girlfriends' boyfriends or ex-boyfriends. Then again, Miss Sandra A. Moore never did abide by any rules, spoken or unspoken. It was as if she made up her own rules to her own haphazard life.

DJ L—S.O.S. placed his hand on Sandy's shoulder and told her, "My dear sister, I'm going to pray over you out loud, but while I'm praying, you need to confess to God right now what you have done to cause your relationship with Him to slip. The crowd doesn't need to hear it and I don't need to hear it, but you need to whisper it loud enough so you and God hear, because the Word of God says in 1 John 1:9 that if we confess our sins—and the word *confess* means to say—then he is faithful and just to forgive us our sins and cleanse us from all unrighteousness." DJ L—S.O.S. proceeded to pray for Sandy as I just looked at him praying for her, wishing he would throw some of that prayer over on me. I was the one standing in the need of prayer at this point. Sandy was just a bag of emotion responding to guilt, while I was the one secretly dying on the inside. As the DJ prayed, I could hear Sandy pray but couldn't make out exactly what she said. I wondered what else she prayed about, what other sins she had to confess and what other boyfriends of other women she had messed with. Matthew? *Where is Liz, anyway?* I asked myself as I looked around the room for her once again. If there was ever a time I needed my best friend with me, I sure did need her now.

Next thing you know, a group of female prayer warriors encircled Sandy and prayed loudly for her, as Sandy kept bawling out of control. I stepped back ten steps and let the praying women take over and just looked at the girl with a mixture of shock and utter disgust. I couldn't believe these people were falling for her little tantrum.

Not being able to take it anymore, I turned around, burst through the crowd, dashed out the door and raced toward my Taurus parked on the street with hopes that no one would see me before I got inside and cried my eyes out.

As I almost reached my destination, I was stopped by a familiar voice calling after me. "Michelle!"

I stopped dead in my tracks, turned around abruptly and wiped away any tears before they were able to form. "Not now, David!" I yelled. Now, why did he have to follow me out? He picks the worst times to try and get my attention.

Instead of retreating back inside the party, David caught up with me, out of breath. "Michelle, what's wrong? Why'd you storm out of there? Didn't you see Sandy crying at the front?"

"None of your business, David, okay!" I snapped. I didn't feel like hearing any sermon about how I'm supposed to be there for people in their time of need and console them and love them regardless.

"Whoa, I'm sorry." David backed up with his hands raised in the air. "Didn't mean to butt in on anything major. I just wanted to make sure everything was all right with you."

David then paused and said, "You know I still care about you."

*Oh, no, no no, David.* I shook my head and covered my face with my hands so as not to show him I was about to cry. I couldn't understand why I was so emotional on this brisk night in June. My period must be coming on this week, because my emotions were going crazy. At that moment I wished I could just click my heels three times and be home, as if I were Dorothy from *The Wiz.*

*There's no place like home…there's no place like home….*

"David," I began in a much softer tone this time. "I know you care about me," I said with a crackling voice. "I just— I don't need this right now."

"I know, I know. I'll get out of your way," David said and backed up, turned around and headed back to the party entrance.

Before he went back inside he faced me again and said, "Just let me know if you need anything. I'll be here."

I thought about David's last words as he closed the door behind him. I wished I could take him up on his offer. I definitely needed something. I needed prayer. I needed a healing for my soul. I needed rest in the middle of a storm, peace of mind. I needed Jesus. *Sweet Jesus, please help me through this.* I felt like an emotional train wreck and I couldn't take it anymore.

Once I made it inside my car, I actually thought for a moment about going back inside and checking on Sandy before I left. Even though she slept with my ex, I still couldn't deny that I cared about her wild butt. I wondered if Sandy would ever learn that she needs to love God more than she should ever love man and that she needs to put God first and foremost and stop making immature mistakes. The girl has been saved well over a year. She should know better by now.

She needs to grow up! Maybe this time, if I'm not there for her to clean up after her mess, it will finally prove to her once and for all that life isn't just one big party and that there are consequences to one's inconsiderate, selfish, careless actions.

So my mind's made up. No, I will not go and rescue her this time. This time she's going to have to deal with this mess she got herself into on her own. I started the ignition and drove off.

# Chapter 28

*Revelation*

Matthew followed after Liz, who was still standing in a frozen position on the sidewalk. She turned around to face him. "She's your what?"

"She's my sister."

Those words stung Liz's ears and she felt as if she was in the middle of a nightmare.

"Well, my half sister."

"I didn't know you had a half sister."

"I know. She's from Ohio, and we weren't that close until now. She's pregnant and she's only sixteen and has been too afraid to tell her mom or our dad. Somehow she found out her older brother was a minister, so she sought me out, used all that she had to catch a bus here and told only me about the pregnancy. She confided in me, Liz, and told me not to tell anyone. I told her I wouldn't, but that I would eventually let her parents know before she went back home. It was also then that I was going to let you know...we just hadn't gotten to that point yet."

Liz felt lower than low. She felt like crawling underneath a rock. She'd been so mean and so hurtful to Matthew and that young girl. Liz was ashamed.

"So, Liz, you were right. There is another woman. There is another woman whose place to stay I'm paying for and who I've been coming around to, bringing groceries and taking care of and ministering to well into the night. That other woman is my baby sister, Ms. Elizabeth Coleman."

"Matthew, I'm so sorry. I didn't know," Liz said.

"I know you didn't know," Matthew continued. "Which is why you need to ask before you go off assuming things and questioning my character!" Matthew yelled in anger.

Liz was stunned.

"Liz, you got issues, and I don't think I have enough patience to deal with your jealous, accusatory ways in a relationship. So I agree with you—it *is* over. It's been over for me for a while now. I just kept wanting to wait it out, hoping and praying that a considerate, caring side of you would eventually show forth, but that never happened. It never happened, Liz. So I think that our being apart is the best for the both of us. I bid you godspeed and goodbye."

And with that, Matthew walked back inside the apartment building, not looking back, leaving Liz sulking on the sidewalk. Liz held her head down and slowly walked back to her ride.

She got in the car, turned the ignition, then suddenly balled her hand into a fist and slammed it hard into the steering wheel and cried in her hands.

# Chapter 29

*The Houseguest*

Liz was rudely awakened the next morning to the sound of someone bamming on the front door. She got up, threw on her dingy white robe, then headed to the front room to see who in the world would be banging on the door like a maniac at five o'clock on a Sunday morning. She had hoped whoever it was didn't wake up baby Joshua, who was sound asleep in the crib in Ms. Coleman's bedroom.

Ms. Coleman had beaten Liz to the front door, tied the belt of her black satin robe in a bow and looked through the peephole.

Ms. Coleman spotted a fair-skinned, forty-something woman wearing a red satin scarf on her head, which also had light brown hair and pink sponge rollers sticking out on the sides.

"Who is it, Mom?" Liz asked.

"I don't know, but whoever it is, she looks like some wild woman standing on the porch."

*Bam! Bam! Bam! Bam! Bam!*

Ms. Coleman jumped up as the continuous banging on the door startled her.

"Who is it?" Ms. Coleman finally asked.

"It's your worst nightmare!" the woman yelled from the porch. "And I suggest you open the door before I come in there after you, you home wrecker!"

"Earnestine Miller," Ms. Coleman said softly to herself, loud enough for Liz to hear.

"Earnestine? Richard's wife?" Liz asked. "What in the world is she doing over here?"

Ms. Coleman faced her daughter. "I don't know. She must be looking for Richard."

"Now open the door, tramp!" Earnestine yelled from the porch. "I know you're in there! I see your beady and shifty eyes looking through the peephole!"

"Good ole Richard must not have come home last night, otherwise this crazy woman wouldn't be over here looking for him," Liz said.

"I guess," Ms. Coleman agreed. "Richard ain't here, if that's who you're looking for!" she yelled through the door, hoping that would be enough to make Earnestine leave the premises.

"You liar! I hear him in there!" Earnestine shouted.

Liz and Ms. Coleman gave each other confused glances. Maybe she mistook the sounds from the TV for her husband, Liz thought.

"Now open the door!" Earnestine demanded while punching her statement with swear words.

"You want me to call the cops?" Liz asked. She had had enough of this nonsense. She was ready to go back to bed, as she only had a few hours left to snooze before she got up to get ready for church, as she'd had a long night last night.

"Earnestine, I promise you, Richard is not here! I haven't talked to nor seen Richard in over six months. He ain't here!" Ms. Coleman yelled at the top of her lungs.

"Why don't you let me come in there and see for myself?" Earnestine asked in a more rational tone this time, as if she'd suddenly turned into a nice person.

Ms. Coleman paused for a moment.

"Mom, don't do it," Liz pleaded. "That woman is crazy. No telling what she would do."

Ms. Coleman kept thinking about whether or not she should let her in, when suddenly she unbolted the lock and opened the door.

Earnestine burst through the door and started searching the house as if she were the police.

"Okay, now where is he?" Earnestine asked as she waltzed in the kitchen, then looked underneath the kitchen sink. She left the kitchen, then started opening closet doors. "Where is that no-good son of a—"

"Earnestine," Ms. Coleman cut her off. "Like I said before, Richard is not here. Now, I didn't have to let you in here, so I'm going to ask that you respect my house by not going through it like you have a search warrant!"

Earnestine waltzed right up to Ms. Coleman and looked her dead in her chocolate face. "I didn't know you were his type," Earnestine snarled.

"Woman, you betta get outta my face before I—" Ms. Coleman said through clenched teeth.

"Before you what? What you gonna do about it, you little pint-size home wrecker?" Earnestine said while pointing in Ms. Coleman's face. "What you gonna do?"

"Ladies, ladies," Liz intervened. "There's no need for all this!" she said as she came between the women before something really went down.

Liz knew how her mother could get sometimes, saved or unsaved, if anybody put their fingers in her face, so she was trying to spare Ms. Earnestine a world of trouble and pain.

"Earnestine, I'm telling you the God-honest truth, I don't know where your husband is. He left me right after he found out I was—" Ms. Coleman paused because she'd forgotten that she hadn't told this woman that she had a baby by her husband.

"Found out you were what?" Earnestine asked.

"Found out I was pregnant with his son."

"His son? Why you little—" Earnestine dived on top of Ms. Coleman, and Liz grabbed her off her just in time and held the woman by the waist as her arms went flailing wildly in the air.

Earnestine proceeded to call Ms. Coleman every name in the book as Ms. Coleman stood there with her arms extended toward her, praying in tongues and attempting to cast a demon out.

Just then a breaking news story chimed in from the television.

"This just in," the anchorwoman said as the previous church program was interrupted. "There has been a fatal pileup accident on I-75 as a truck driver apparently fell asleep at the wheel and crashed into the shoulder, causing vehicles to crash into the back of it, resulting in a domino effect, leaving four dead and several wounded."

Liz, Ms. Coleman and Earnestine watched the news with their mouths open as they watched the scene of the accident showing several cars piled on top of each other, police sirens and smoke. It looked like a scene out of an action film, let alone an actual occurrence on a major local freeway.

The anchorwoman continued, "Those confirmed dead include Thomas Chokerman, Elizabeth Little, Kathy Roman and Richard Miller."

"Richard!" Earnestine screamed hysterically, then started shaking wildly and crying like a baby. "Not my Richard!" she cried. "They can't mean my Richard!"

Ms. Coleman and Liz stared in shock at the TV and tears like rivers flowed from Ms. Coleman's cheeks once they showed a picture of the victims on-screen, confirming that the Richard who was no more was indeed Earnestine's wandering husband and baby Joshua's father.

Earnestine wept and wailed as if she'd lost her only child as tears flooded her eyes. Liz grabbed a box of Kleenex and handed it to her, and she grabbed several pieces and blew her nose.

"Not my Richard! Not my Richard!" she kept saying over and over.

Ms. Coleman sat in shock as the man she'd once loved and had a baby by was now dead. Even though he'd left her cold, she still loved the man.

Ms. Coleman matched Earnestine's tears, grabbed and held her and rocked her from side to side.

More important than Ms. Coleman's feeling of loss for her baby's father, she felt sorry for the woman she held in her arms who'd obviously loved this man more than she ever could.

"Not my Richard! Not my Richard!" Earnestine continued. "Dear God, why?"

Suddenly a shrieking cry came from Ms. Coleman's bedroom.

All of the excitement going on in the front room must have awakened baby Joshua, as he screamed hysterically, in desperate need of attention.

Ms. Coleman and Liz exchanged glances as Liz said, "I'll check on him," and arose from her seat.

Ms. Coleman continued to rock Earnestine. Then Earnestine looked up at Ms. Coleman, wiped her tears and asked, "Can I see him?"

Ms. Coleman was surprised that this woman wanted to see her child, the one who was a spitting image of his now-deceased father. Maybe she believed by seeing him it would somehow allow her to have one last look at her husband—or what he'd left behind.

Ms. Coleman arose from the couch and Earnestine followed her into the bedroom.

Inside the bedroom the two women watched Liz hold and rock baby Joshua, who was wrapped in a blue baby blanket. Joshua smiled at Liz with dimming eyes as she sang a soulful yet sweet rendition of "Jesus Loves Me." Liz hadn't realized she had an audience until she turned around and saw Ms. Coleman and Earnestine standing at the doorway.

"You always could sing," Ms. Coleman told her daughter. "When I try to sing to Joshua, he starts crying. I don't know where you got your singing voice from. You sure didn't get it from me," Ms. Coleman said with a slight laugh.

Liz turned the baby toward Earnestine, who stood in awe at the sight Liz held in her arms, and asked, "Wanna see him?"

Earnestine walked up to baby Joshua and stared at him. She was amazed at how much he resembled his father. She wiggled his little nose with her finger, and baby Joshua opened his eyes wide and smiled at her.

Earnestine smiled in return, then her smile turned into tears.

Ms. Coleman laid her head on the shoulder of Earnestine, who then laid her head on Liz's back as Liz continued to rock baby Joshua back to sleep.

Ms. Coleman extended her arms and gave both women a warm embrace as they shared the pain of death and the joy of life—together.

# Chapter 30

*Speak to My Heart*

Relieved that I finally made it inside, I threw my purse on the kitchen table, plopped on the brown couch, then cried hysterically in my hands. At least I am free to bawl like this when I'm alone. This way, only I and God know how I really feel, and I am free to wail like a baby with no one else seeing me or passing judgment, wondering, *Why is Michelle crying? I thought she was so strong.* This way, no one will ever know that I'm sensitive, that sometimes I get weak and that every now and then I just need a good cry.

I cried for what seemed like eternity as I thought about tonight's ordeal. I still couldn't get over the fact that Sandy would betray me like she did. After all I've done for her? After all the times I been there for her, forsaking my own sleep so I could stay up with her praying all night so she could have peace of mind? Lord knows I have come to her rescue on more than one occasion. I've prayed for her, I've been her spiritual guide and mentor, but, more importantly, I've been a true friend to that girl...how could she do this to me?

Then again, maybe it wasn't even her fault. I'm sure Pierre was the one who initiated everything. I can't see Sandy's weak self personally setting out to hurt my feelings. I'm sure Pierre gave her some lame excuse as to why he needed to see her, and Sandy, like a fool, fell for it. Whatever he said definitely did the trick, because she somehow ended up at his house and in his bed.

His bed.

I can remember that waterbed like I saw it yesterday. I remember when I first saw that bed when I went over his house while we were dating one Saturday afternoon because he claimed, after we were already out and about, that he left his jacket at home and that he needed to go back and get it because he was cold. He asked me to wait for him inside his place while he looked for his jacket. If you ask me, I think he just wanted me to see what his place looked like. I must admit, it did look nice. He definitely had a flair for interior decorating. As I observed his black-and-silver decor that day, I can remember thinking how it seemed to have taken forever for him to find that doggone jacket.

I eventually had to use it, so I asked him where his bathroom was. He told me it was down the hall, to the left, but when I opened the door that was down the hall, to the left, I didn't see any toilet stool or shower curtain—I saw his bedroom. His large bedroom, with that king-size waterbed with the leopard comforter.

I stood frozen while being mesmerized by the bed. I wanted to touch it, feel it or maybe lay my body down and roll in it. The last time I was in a waterbed, I was eleven years old with my mom at a furniture store and the salesman showed Mom their waterbeds for sale. Even then I plopped on the bed as a child and allowed the waves to seemingly take me away as I rolled around and got lost in the sheets.

As I stood staring at Pierre's waterbed that day two years ago, I wondered how exactly did I end up at his bedroom? I walked down the hall and headed to the left, like he said. But clearly this was no bathroom.

Pierre walked up on me and grabbed me from behind as I continued to stare at his bed. "Like what you see?" he asked, then moved my hair to the side and started kissing my neck. Instead of shoving him away, I tilted my head, closed my eyes and imagined Pierre picking me up and carrying me to his waterbed and the two of us rolling around while exploring one another's bodies.

Not surrendering to my own premature fantasy, I immediately opened my eyes and asked, "Did you find your jacket?"

He said he did and we left on our way to the movie theater.

I shook myself from the remembrance of that day. And to think that that was the same waterbed he'd wanted to have me on he went ahead and took Sandy. That was supposed to have been *our* waterbed! We were supposed

to share that waterbed the night after I told him "I do."
Even though I knew, since my introduction to his waterbed
at his place, that he had since proposed to Erika, called off
the wedding, asked me back in his life and I'd told him no,
there was always that slim possibility that we would one day
be together.

In a way, I was looking forward to our rendezvous in that
bed. It was as if that bed always had my name on it. Apparently
not anymore. And to think, he'd claimed to love me
so. For a second I was even starting to believe it this time
when he said he did. I was starting to believe that the
reason he'd called off the wedding to Erika was because he
just might have wanted to be with me instead. But it turns
out he didn't want me. He wanted Sandy! He wanted my
friend! What a loser!

I started crying all over again until I got a headache. The
worst part of all this is wondering, why do I care so much?
Does this mean I still love him or something? *Please, Lord,
no! Lord, please help me get over this man.* He obviously doesn't
love me. And I don't want to love someone who doesn't
love me the way I need to be loved in return. *Lord, please
make my feelings for him go away. Please make me strong. If this
is what love is supposed to feel like, then I don't want it, Lord! I
don't want it!*

I grabbed my small Bible from off the glass coffee table,
thought about opening it to a passage of scripture but instead
threw it back on the table. I didn't even feel like looking in
the Bible. I didn't feel like reading about Jesus or His disciples
or the Old Testament. I didn't feel like being the "good"

Christian who runs to the Bible for and about everything. I wanted someone or something to come to me for a change. I needed God to meet me where I am right now.

"Why did this happen to me, Lord?" I yelled in my apartment. "Why did this happen? Am I *nothing* to the both of them?" I asked, with no reply. "I thought I was everything to them, but I guess I'm nothing."

I curled myself into a little ball on the couch, clutched my legs and rocked myself from side to side in an attempt to regain total peace.

I closed my eyes and waited.

I waited and waited and waited.

I was waiting to hear something—*anything;* I needed a Word from God.

I didn't feel like searching scripture, I didn't feel like praying in tongues to stir something up on the inside and I didn't feel like confessing victory or even praising His holy Name.

I just felt like I needed a Word from God and that if I didn't get it tonight, I would just go crazy.

*Be still, My child,* the Lord spoke to my spirit. *Be still and listen to your Heavenly Father.* I kept rocking from side to side, ready to receive divine Words from Him.

*Know that I am with you always. I am with you even unto the end of the world. I will never leave you nor forsake you.*

I smiled to myself. I loved it when Daddy reminded me He is always here for me, even in the midst of my temper tantrums.

*I see your tears and I see your pain,* the Lord continued

speaking to my heart. *Know that weeping may endure for a moment, but joy cometh in the morning.*

That line sounded familiar. I guess it was time for me to receive it for myself.

*So dry your eyes, trust and believe,* God continued. *Trust and believe in the love that I have for thee. Trust and believe in the grace I have given thee. Trust and believe in the mercy I have given thee. And as I have given mercy to thee, which is new every morning, I want you to extend that same grace to others. For blessed are the merciful, for they shall obtain mercy.*

What? God threw me off with that last statement. Is *this* my Word from God? Is this the Word I had been waiting for all this time? Give grace and mercy to others? But what about me, Lord? I'm tired of always giving to others. What about me? *I'm* the one who's hurting here! *I'm* the one who was betrayed! Why is it that I'm the one who always has to show grace and mercy? Why do I always have to give? When will I get to experience total victory, instead of always having to be everyone's shoulder to cry on? Where is my shoulder to cry on? I have needs, too, God!

For several minutes I heard no response from my Heavenly Father. Not hearing from Him in response to my cry for help felt like the loneliest place in the world. He must understand where I'm coming from. If anyone would understand, I just knew God would. I mean, I know I'm supposed to forgive and all, but at that very moment I just didn't want to. I couldn't imagine forgiving Pierre and Sandy and just moving on just like nothing happened. They don't deserve to be forgiven, anyway. Their two pitiful selves belonged with each other because they're both selfish, self-centered and emotionally draining.

After still not hearing a reply from God, I cried silently to myself. I realized what I had just done. I'd yelled at God. For some reason, deep down, I was somehow mad at Him. I was mad at Him for allowing this to happen to me. I was mad at Him for telling me I need to forgive them when they were the ones who'd hurt me. It was as if He favored them more than me, and here I am, the one trying to live holy and do things according to His will, while still ending up being the one who is hurt, angry and all alone.

I know that I have God and that I'm never alone with Him, but, Lord, when am I going to have a husband? Why is it that when I obey You or think I'm obeying You, things still don't turn out right or in my favor? I want a husband, like, yesterday, Lord. Here I am almost thirty and still not married. Here I am serving the Lord with my whole heart and still experiencing heartache and pain. It's just not fair, Lord! It's not fair!

Still not having received the answers I wanted, I stretched out on the couch, placed my hand underneath my head as a pillow and fell asleep.

# Chapter 31

*At Last*

Sandy finally made it home from the party at one in the morning. So as to not awaken Madear, she tiptoed to her bedroom, quietly closed the door behind her and changed into her satin pink pajamas. Instead of immediately going to sleep, she grabbed her brown fuzzy teddy bear off her pillow, sat on the floor beside her bed and squeezed Teddy real tight.

Even though she believed the words of those praying for her at the party—comforting words which assured her that because she had confessed her sin before God, God had truly forgiven her and how, as far as the east is from the west, He will no longer remember her sins—Sandy thought about the one she'd hurt in the process, her one and only true friend, Michelle.

Tears slowly rolled down Sandy's face as she thought about the pain she must have caused her. She cried even more as she thought about how Michelle had trusted her, as her friend, not to betray her, but how she'd behaved more selfishly simply because she'd wanted the attention and affection of a man she'd thought was worthy of her time.

She thought about how much she'd wanted Pierre and had been even more delighted to know that he'd wanted her in return. To Sandy, Pierre was the most saved man she knew, and she'd somehow convinced herself that since Michelle no longer wanted him, he was free to be with anyone. She'd never thought that getting the man she wanted would cause a friendship to come to an end—until the man she wanted happened to be her best friend's ex-boyfriend.

Sandy heard tapping and looked up at the door and immediately hopped up from the floor. She didn't want Madear to catch her sitting and crying on the floor because she knew Madear would wonder what was wrong.

"Can I come in?" Madear asked from outside the door.

Sandy drew the covers off her once made-up bed, acting as if she was about to lie down in it, and said, "Sure."

"I heard you when you came in," Madear said.

Sandy looked at Madear strangely as she wondered how in the world Madear could hear her come in when she'd made every attempt possible so as to not awaken her.

"So how was the party?" Madear asked and plopped on the edge of Sandy's bed before Sandy could lie in it herself.

Sandy walked over to the vanity set and adjusted the

makeup and nail polish so as to not gain eye contact with her grandmother. She didn't want her to notice her bloodshot red eyes, stained from crying.

"It was fine," Sandy said.

"So tell me about it!" Madear said excitedly and clapped her hands together.

Sandy wondered why Madear was up this late, for one, and why she was acting all chipper, as though it was one in the afternoon instead of one in the morning.

"There really is nothing to tell," Sandy said and headed to her closet, acting as if she was looking for an outfit. "We went, we danced, we had a good time, and that was it!"

"That was it, huh?" Madear probed.

Sandy got fed up, turned to face her grandmother and snapped, "Yes, Madear, that was it! What else do you want me to tell you?"

Madear looked up at her grandchild and calmly said, "The truth."

Sandy couldn't take it anymore. She turned into a bowl of jelly and started bawling like a baby, crying in her hands, reliving the whole experience all over again.

Madear arose from the bed, grabbed Sandy's head and planted it inside her plump chest.

"Shhhhhh," Madear said. "It's okay, baby, it's okay."

Sandy kept crying in Madear's chest, then said in a muffled tone, "What's wrong with me, Madear? What's wrong with me?"

"It's okay, baby, it's okay," Madear repeated while rocking

Sandy from side to side. She walked Sandy over to the bed and the two of them sat on the edge, with Sandy wiping her drenched eyes with the back of her hands.

"Now tell me what happened tonight," Madear asked again, this time ready to receive the whole story.

"I rededicated my life back to God tonight," Sandy said while twiddling her thumbs.

"Well, praise the Lord, that's a good thing, baby!" Madear said and patted Sandy's hand.

"Yeah," Sandy said, then wiped another tear. "Well, the reason I rededicated my life back to God is because the other night I spent the night at Pierre's house."

"Oh," Madear said.

"I mean, we didn't have sex or anything, but we kissed each other all night long. You know Pierre—Michelle's ex-boyfriend?"

"Well, I do remember that name," Madear said while looking up at the sky, trying to place a face with the name.

"Well, anyway, tonight at the party they had an altar call, and I felt the Lord leading me to respond and repent…so I did."

"Well, that's a good thing, baby. It shows that you're remorseful and that you're ready to receive God's loving arms of forgiveness once again."

"I know. You're right," Sandy said with lowered eyes. "But Michelle was with me when I did, and I kinda told her what happened."

"Oh," Madear said.

"And she kinda wasn't too happy about it."

"I'm sure she wasn't, baby. From when I used to hear you talk about the two of them when they were together, it sounded like they were in love. I used to think they were going to get married one day. So, yes, she has a right to be upset," Madear said assuredly.

Sandy looked on the floor and tears welled up in her eyes once again.

Madear grabbed Sandy's right hand and looked her dead in the eye, "Now, Sandy, Michelle is going to be upset at first, but eventually she'll forgive you—but that's if, and only if, you ask her for her forgiveness. Have you asked her for her forgiveness?" Madear asked.

Sandy thought about that for a second. For some reason she'd thought asking God to forgive her was enough. She'd never thought about asking Michelle for her forgiveness, as well.

"No," she replied.

"Well, you should ask her to forgive you. It's not enough to ask God," Madear said, leading Sandy to believe that Madear was reading her mind. "You also want to ask for forgiveness from those you have hurt and done wrong," Madear said, then kissed her grandbaby on the forehead and added, "It's going to be okay, baby."

Madear then arose from the bed, said, "You get some sleep now, all right?" and left the room.

Sandy thought about what Madear had told her and concluded she was absolutely right. She wondered if it was too late for her to call Michelle, seeing as though it was almost two in the morning. However, Sandy decided that she couldn't sleep unless she knew, without a shadow of a doubt, that her one true friend, the one who always had her back, the one who had always been there for her and the one who understood her more than anybody else, had forgiven her.

Sandy picked up her cell from off the nightstand and hurriedly dialed Michelle's number.

After five rings Michelle's voice mail came on.

Sandy decided against leaving a long, drawn-out voice mail, so she dialed her number again.

This time after the third ring a sleepy voice answered the phone.

"Hello?"

"Michelle, this is Sandy—"

*Click.*

Sandy just stared at the phone.

She couldn't believe Michelle had just hung up on her. *Maybe she was just tired,* Sandy thought. Then she thought a minute and thought to herself, *Or maybe she hasn't forgiven me and never will.*

Sandy tried to call Michelle's number again while another call was trying to come in on her phone at the same time. Sandy looked at the caller ID and saw that it was Pierre.

"Hello?" Sandy answered, surprised to hear from him again.

"Hey, beautiful, how are you doing?"

"I'm fine," Sandy said sweetly. In the midst of her current debacle, she was actually glad to hear his smooth-sounding voice once again.

"That's good. Hey, I was wondering what you were doing tonight?" Pierre asked, sounding half-asleep himself.

"Tonight?" Sandy asked. "You mean this morning?" she said in reference to the fact that it *was* after two o'clock.

"Tonight, this morning—whatever," Pierre said. After a slight pause he added, "I need you."

"You need me?" Sandy asked. Even though she liked the way that sounded, she was still a little suspicious. "You need me for what?"

"I need you here by my side. Ever since you left, I couldn't stop thinking about you."

Sandy held the phone closer to her ear and smiled.

"I haven't been able to sleep," he said. "And when I tried to sleep last night, I had nightmares."

"Nightmares?" Sandy asked.

"Yes, nightmares. But I know if you were here with me, that would make all those nightmares go away."

Sandy held the phone for a minute.

Suddenly her future flashed before her eyes. Pierre. Lifelong love. House full of beautiful kids. She felt this may be her one and only chance to make her dream of true love and happiness come true.

*Who's to say that Michelle will ever forgive me?* Sandy thought. *She sure didn't sound ready to forgive me when she just hung up in my face. Friendships don't last always, but a shot at true love may only come once in a lifetime.* As for right now, Sandy concluded, her man needed her. He needed her to be there right by his side—right now.

"I'll be there in a minute," Sandy said and hung up the phone.

She got dressed in some tight jeans and a pink baby tee and packed a small gym bag with her pajamas and toiletries.

She was headed out the door when she was suddenly stopped.

"Where do you think you're going, young lady?" Madear asked sternly, arms folded, leaning against the wall in the front room.

"Out. Something came up and I gotta check on something."

"Something came up, huh, at two in the morning?" Madear asked.

"Yeah, Madear, something came up! Now will you stop bugging me all the time and just get out of my life!" Sandy had had it up to here with Madear's prying into her personal business.

"Sandy, dear, the only things open this late are legs and bars, and the last time I checked, you sure wasn't no bar hopper."

"Look, Madear, I gotta go," Sandy said, then reached toward the doorknob.

"Sandy, chile, if you walk out that door right now, don't plan on coming back!" Madear ordered.

Sandy turned around and looked at her grandmother who'd raised her since she was six years old and said, "You know what? That sounds like a great idea to me!" She then opened the door, slammed it shut, backed out of the driveway like a whirlwind and sped down the neighborhood street.

Pierre softly stroked Sandy's short black tresses as she lay in his lap on his black leather couch, both of them fully clothed. She was staring up at the ceiling when Pierre said softly in Sandy's ear in a sultry tone, "Sandy, baby, I'm so glad you're here with me tonight. For a minute there I thought I lost you."

Sandy smiled. It was as if he was reading her mind, because for a moment she had thought to herself, what in the world was she doing back at this man's house again? Even though she knew deep down what she was doing may not be right, it sure felt right to her.

Being in Pierre's arms once again and allowing him to play with her hair was somewhat therapeutic.

"What made you think that?" Sandy asked, curious at his response.

Pierre went from rubbing Sandy's hair to rubbing her bare arms and replied, "Well, let's see. I said some things to you before I didn't mean to say. And I want you to know I'm sorry."

Hearing a man admit he was wrong sure sounded good to Sandy. However, she couldn't quite remember what he was apologizing for, except maybe for allowing her to walk right out the door, with him acting as though he didn't care. *That must be it,* Sandy thought.

"That's okay, baby," Sandy cooed and looked up at Pierre. "I forgive you," she said and smiled.

"Girl!" Pierre yelled suddenly.

"What?" Sandy replied while laughing at the same time.

"You are just so fine! My God!" Pierre said, then gave Sandy a tight squeeze.

Sandy started laughing louder. "Thanks, Pierre, you're so sweet." Her look then grew solemn.

After a brief, uncomfortable silence, Pierre asked, "What's wrong, gorgeous?"

"Do you really like me, Pierre?" Sandy asked. She felt as if she needed to know now more than ever.

"Do I like you?" Pierre asked in shock, wondering why he was even asked that question. "Do I like you?" Pierre asked again. "Girl, you mean the *world* to me!" he assured her.

"Are you just saying that because…"

"Because what?" Pierre asked.

"Because I'm not Michelle?"

Pierre let out a huge sigh. "Is that what this is all about?"

Sandy looked up at Pierre, waiting for a response.

"Sandra A. Moore, the fact that you're *not* Michelle is the main reason I like you so much. The two of you are totally different, and I like that about you, girl!"

"In what way?" Sandy probed.

"Well…" Pierre thought for a moment. "Michelle's so stiff sometimes. And boring. And she acts so holier than thou like she's Miss Hype for Jesus USA or something."

Sandy laughed out loud.

"But you, Sandy, you're so sweet and fun and outgoing."

Sandy looked up at Pierre and he added with bedroom eyes, "You keep the fire burning inside of me."

Pierre's face drew closer to Sandy as he was about to kiss her, when Sandy suddenly announced, "Madear threw me out of the house tonight."

"She did what?" Pierre asked in shock.

"She kicked me out."

"Why?" Pierre asked.

"I don't know," Sandy said hesitatingly, "but I think I have a clue."

"What is it?" he asked, unsure himself.

"I think she threw me out because she knows I'm here, right now, with you."

"Oh," Pierre said quietly.

"Am I wrong for being here with you right now?" Sandy asked Pierre while staring up at the ceiling. "Am I wrong for being here, lying in your big, strong arms?" Sandy asked. Her mind grew clouded. She was confused.

"Does it feel wrong?" Pierre whispered in her ear.

Sandy didn't respond.

"Am I wrong for feeling for you the way that I do?" Pierre added while allowing his hands to go from stroking her bare arms to finding their way underneath her shirt and circling her belly button.

Sandy kept quiet and closed her eyes.

"Am I wrong for loving you?" Pierre whispered in Sandy's ear.

"You don't love me," Sandy whispered, eyes still shut.

"I do, Sandy, baby, I do," Pierre cooed.

"You're just saying that so you can—"

"Move in with me," Pierre suggested out of the blue.

Sandy fell silent, wondering if she'd just heard him say what she thought she'd heard.

"Do what?" Sandy said, then sat upright on the couch.

Pierre sat upright, as well, and repeated demandingly, "I said move in with me."

"Move in with you?" Sandy asked in shock.

She hadn't thought she had that as an option. Sure, she hadn't known where she would go, but she'd never thought it would be to live with Pierre.

Pierre then got in front of Sandy and plopped down on one knee. "Sandy, baby, I love you and I want to be with you 24-7."

Sandy couldn't believe it! He was down on his knees! She had always dreamed of this very moment!

"Will you move in with me?" Pierre asked in a boyish tone.

She didn't know how to respond. Sure, it wasn't quite the marriage proposal she'd expected, but it was close enough.

Besides, she had nowhere else to go. Right now she couldn't afford to look for a place to stay since she didn't have any savings—and she seriously doubted that Michelle would be willing to let her live with her at her place.

But still, Sandy wanted to be sure of something before she gave her final answer.

"I don't know," Sandy said, with Pierre still on his knees in front of her. "I mean, what if we get tempted and—"

"Sandy, baby, don't worry about a thing. I'll honor

you. I promise I won't try and sleep with you until after we get married."

*Did he just say "after we get married,"* Sandy thought. *So this moving in together is a prerequisite to our one day getting married? Glory to God, hallelujah!*

Sandy leaped for joy on the inside. Her dream was finally coming true!

In the middle of her thoughts, she almost forgot that there was an anxious man in front of her on his knees, waiting for a response.

"Will you?" Pierre asked again. "I promise I will never leave you nor forsake you, baby."

Hearing Pierre say those last words were like music to Sandy's ears.

Her parents had left her years ago when they'd died in that car accident. Her grandmother had forsaken her when she'd lost faith in her and thrown her out the house. And her friend, whom she considered to be her best friend in the world, had left her crying at the front of a party full of strangers and was now ignoring her calls and hanging up on her. But now here was a man who promised to never leave her side and who was proving that he wanted her there with him all the time by asking her to move in with him. *And* he was promising not to have sex with her until marriage?

Sandy nodded her head up and down in front of Pierre and emphatically replied, "Yes!"

Pierre then hopped up, picked up Sandy and gave her a huge hug and spun her around the front room.

Sandy screamed with delight, as this moment signified

one of the happiest moments in her life. She wasn't sure if she was happy because she now had a place to stay and a man to call her own or because Pierre looked so happy. His outward expression of joy made Sandy even more delighted herself, so much so that she pinched herself to make sure she wasn't dreaming, then laughed out loud. Both their joy and exuberance was confirmation to Sandy that she may be doing the right thing.

After all this time and after all she'd been through, Sandy could finally honestly say that she had found her man of God—or, in other words, he had found her. A man who would love her, a man who would keep and protect her, a man who would never let her go.

# Chapter 32

*Heaven Knows*

I arrived at church in my sharp black-and-white pin-striped pant suit, white silk blouse and white large-brim hat a whole twenty-five minutes late. I didn't care. With all I had gone through with Sandy and Pierre, I'd almost decided not to go to church at all but instead watch service on the Internet. However, I'd remembered that I just got paid on Friday and needed to bring my tithe to the storehouse.

The usher led me to a row with an empty seat in the upper part of the sanctuary. I said, "Excuse me," to those already standing, while trying not to hit anyone with my hat. Lord knows I'm not a fan of sitting in the back, especially when it's normally filled with other latecomers, babies crying and folks who were just not into service and praise and worship like I would like them to be. Sometimes it felt like a whole different congregation sat in the back. But this time I didn't mind because today I felt like being part of that other congregation. The give-me-the-Word-for-the-day-so-I-can-pay-my-tithes-and-go-home congregation. At this point, I didn't care where I sat. I figured the closer I am to the back, the quicker I can head to the exit door once service let out.

After the music selection, Pastor Wilkins made his way to the pulpit, and I arose right along with the congregation. The congregation shouted and praised God and I did the same. Pastor Wilkins introduced a guest minister from out of town, then turned the pulpit over to a handsome, older, charismatic gentleman with a southern drawl and a thick mustache.

After a couple of introductory jokes, the guest minister led us in an opening prayer, then told us to grab our Bibles and wave them at the ground in order to scare the devil and keep him in his place, which is under our feet.

After the demonstration, the minister asked that the congregation be seated and he asked everyone to turn their Bibles to Mark 11:25.

He then began to read. *"And when ye stand praying, forgive, if ye have ought against any, that your Father also which is in heaven may forgive you your trespasses."*

Forgive. Oh, Lord, I'd forgotten about that part. As many times as I'd heard Mark 11:25 quoted at this church, for some reason the word *forgive* stood out today.

The guest minister continued. "So, apparently, here Jesus is adding a condition or a caveat to this initial prayer of faith. Here He is saying, when you stand praying, forgive. When you stand praying, forgive. When you pray, forgive. Those two go hand in hand."

"Amen!" a man shouted from the middle of the congregation.

"Prayer is the ultimate expression of love. In the same sense, forgiveness is an expression of love, as well. For God *so loved* that He gave. But God also *so forgave* mankind that He gave His only begotten Son, if you will. Those two concepts are synonymous. Prayer. Love. Forgiveness. You can't have one without the other."

"Amen!" folks in the congregation agreed.

I must admit, he did have a point. I sat up in my seat.

"Also, saints, now I want you all to hear me on this one...forgiveness is not just about the other person being vindicated. It's not about the other person getting off easy, so to speak."

Huh? Was he talking to me? Who told this guest preacher I had never heard before all my business?

"Forgiveness frees you!" the minister added exuberantly. "Forgiving someone else who has wronged you, misused you, talked about you, lied on you, mistreated you or even took your man from right underneath your nose actually frees you, so you can still have the opportunity to walk in victory!"

The entire congregation laughed, shouted, and some stood up and lifted their hands in praise.

I looked around to make sure no one else noticed my toes being stepped on by this guest preacher.

"How many people can think of somebody right now they need to forgive?"

A sea of hands arose all over the congregation, including mine. I looked around in amazement, shocked to see so many hands possibly experiencing the same thing I was experiencing right now.

"I want you to get up on your feet and we're going to pray for that person we need to forgive," the guest preacher said.

*Excuse me?*

Folks in the congregation hopped to their feet. After minutes of contemplating I slowly but surely arose, as well.

The minister continued, "Okay, now first I want you to think of the person or persons you need to forgive. 'Cause I can sense in my spirit that some of y'all got a whole lot of people y'all need to forgive. I'm talking families, relatives. Even preachers."

I closed my eyes and pictured Sandy's smiling, carefree face. Knowing Sandy, she probably didn't have a clue about how all this was affecting me. I then thought about and relived what happened last night. I saw Sandy keeled over, in tears, at the party, begging for forgiveness from God. Seeing that picture in my mind reminded me that maybe Sandy hadn't meant to hurt me and, more importantly, hurt God.

The minister continued, "Okay, now that you have that person in your mind, I want you to pray for them. Loud and fervently!"

The congregation began to pray. I prayed quietly in tongues while picturing Sandy's face.

"C'mon, louder! I want to hear you pray!" the preacher

demanded. "Pray for that person's life to be blessed! Pray for that person to receive all the best that God has for them. And if that person hurt you so bad that the words of blessing don't seem to want to come out of your mouth, pray in tongues!" the minister added, then laughed. "That way you know you're praying the perfect will of God for their lives, and it keeps you from cursing them out in Jesus' Name."

The congregation grew louder and sounded like a humming machine as everyone prayed fervently in their seats for people who have wronged them in any way.

I balled my hands into two fists and pumped my arms while praying out loud and fervently for Sandy.

After five minutes of praying, the minister then added, "Now I want you to give God a shout of praise for the victory! Praise God for forgiving *you* that day, on the cross at Calvary, freeing your soul from a burning hell. Praise God for giving you Holy Ghost power and the love of God on the inside, which allows you to love somebody else! Praise Him for giving you the love that loves the unlovable and forgives the unforgivable!"

I shouted in victory right along with the entire congregation as the praise team and organist assumed their positions on stage.

"Praise God for loving you and for giving you joy, unspeakable joy, and full of Glory! Praise God for peace in the middle of a storm! Praise God for clothes on your back, food on your table, for waking you up this morning and for keeping you in your right mind!" the preacher said.

The organ struck a chord in between each phrase.

"Praise God, for He's good and His mercy endures forever! You see, forgiveness frees you and forgiveness frees me, and whom the Son sets free is free *indeed!* Hey!"

The organist played a few more chords as the entire congregation starting moving and dancing in their seats. I started jumping up and down in my seat and noticed others leave their seats to go out into the aisle and start dancing. Some even did a lap or two around the sanctuary.

I was so in the flow that eventually I said, "Excuse me," to the people in my row and made my way to the aisle, then I jumped up and down and shouted and praised God harder than I had praised Him in a really long time.

I felt free and alive. My spirit was now awakened, and I felt as if I were supernaturally imparted with the strength to walk in forgiveness with Sandy. My mind was set free, my spirit was set free and my soul was set free! I waved my hands in the air and shouted victory right along with other members in the congregation, other members who, like me, started out sitting in the back but ended up dancing in the aisles.

Immediately after service, I made my way to the lobby and panned the crowd for Sandy. I was so ready to love on her with a big hug and ask her to forgive *me* for being mad at her. I was even willing to maybe go somewhere and sit with her to talk about what had happened and see how this whole fiasco had affected her spiritually and emotionally. I was ready to receive Sandy as one of my closest friends yet once again.

After asking three people if they had seen Sandy and hearing the same response of no, I wondered if Sandy had even made it to church this morning.

"Michelle!" I heard a familiar voice call my name, so I turned around and saw Liz waving her hand in the air, trying to catch my attention. We met each other in the center of the lobby.

"Ooh, girl, look at you, Miss Thang! You are wearing that hat!" Liz said after giving me a light hug.

"Thanks. You lookin' pretty sharp yourself," I said in reference to Liz's canary two-piece suit. "Have you seen Sandy?" I asked, still looking around the lobby.

"Sandy? No, I haven't seen her this morning. She normally comes in the lobby to meet us after service," Liz replied.

"I know, which is why I find it weird that I don't see her."

"She probably didn't make it today," Liz said.

"Maybe, but that's not like her. She normally comes to church practically every Sunday," I said.

"Well, maybe something came up," Liz concluded. "You know, Michelle, not everybody is like you when it comes to church attendance."

I had to pause and think about that last comment. If only Liz knew that earlier this morning I was this close to not coming to church at all.

"I guess," I said, "but I still want to check. I'm about to call her." I lifted the flap of my small white leather purse, grabbed my silver cell phone and dialed Sandy's cell number. Her phone rang and rang and eventually went to voice mail.

"She's not here, Michelle, goodness," Liz said. "Hey, girl, we got some best-friend-to-best-friend catching up to do anyway."

"Why? What's up?" I asked and placed my cell back in my purse.

"It's about Matthew and Mom. Wanna go to breakfast or something so we can talk?"

Uh-oh. It must be pretty serious, since Liz isn't normally the one open to talk nor initiate an after-church discussion over a meal.

"Okay. We can talk," I said. "But I'm not feeling breakfast. Can we meet at Starbucks down the street instead?"

"That's fine," Liz said, and we agreed to meet each other there in the next fifteen minutes.

"I can't believe you and Matthew broke up," I said while sipping on a caramel latte with extra whipped cream. I never thought I would ever see the day that Liz and Matthew were no longer an item. They seemed so perfect for each other.

"I can't believe it either, girl," Liz said while eating a forkful of a low-fat blueberry muffin. "I can't believe how stupid I acted—spying on him, harassing him on the phone, questioning him like he was a common criminal, lying to his face in order to catch him red-handed. It's no wonder he dumped me. I would have dumped me, too."

I tried to understand what she'd just said. "According to what you just told me, Liz, you dumped him first," I reminded her.

"I did, I guess. But that was when I thought he was cheating on me! I didn't know she was his sister."

"But that's the thing, Liz—you *didn't* know, so you shouldn't have assumed—"

"Look, I know this, all right! I already learned my lesson! I was stupid, I was dumb and I just lost probably the best thing that ever happened to me—next to Jesus, of course," Liz said, then placed her hand on her head and looked downward.

I had no idea how much pain this whole ordeal was causing my best friend. If I didn't know any better, I would say that she must have been in love with him. I had never seen Liz look so down and out before. She must have really cared for him.

"Liz, the guest minister preached a good Word today, didn't he?" I said in an attempt to lighten things up a bit.

Liz unhid herself from her hands. "Yeah. And?"

"The word actually freed me on the inside as he spoke about forgiveness," I said.

"Yeah, it was a good word," Liz said, probably wondering why I was bringing up church after she'd just poured her heart out.

"He had us pray for those we need to forgive, and I definitely prayed for Sandy about what I told you she did when we first came in here."

"Yeah, well, she definitely needs prayer."

"I plan on asking Sandy to forgive me even though she hurt me by doing what she did to me," I said.

"That's very big of you, Michelle," Liz said, then stirred her hot chocolate. "Now me, on the other hand, I'm not sure if I would have been so quick to forgive."

"Yeah, well, it's not my doing. The power to forgive Sandy actually came from God. This morning, as I prayed for Sandy, I felt the love of God take over me, which, in a weird way, overtook me and made me into this forgiving person. Before church, I had no intentions on forgiving Sandy. Lord knows I didn't. But after receiving that Word on forgiveness from that guest preacher, I felt empowered to forgive. It sort of reminds me of that scripture that says, 'I can do all things through Christ Jesus,'" I said.

"Oh, yeah? Well, good for you," Liz said, apparently uninterested in what I had to say.

After a slight pause I added, "Maybe you should ask Matthew to forgive you."

Liz said nothing and looked out the window. She saw an expectant mother holding hands with what appeared to be her young son down the street. The two of them looked so happy, so content.

"I don't know, Michelle," Liz finally responded. "Matthew seemed pretty upset about what I did and he actually told me he had been ready to check out of the relationship a long time ago."

"Oh," I said. I hadn't known he was already thinking about ending the relationship. I'd thought everything was smooth sailing with the two of them. Then again, Liz left me out of so much when it came to her private life I feel like I don't hear about anything until it's too late.

"What's wrong with me, Michelle?" Liz asked.

I had never seen Liz look so vulnerable. I was at a loss for words, which is definitely unusual for me. Miss Always

Ready to Dish Advice was speechless. Probably because my own love life had holes in it. I found it hard to give advice to someone else when my own personal life was going down the tubes, as well.

Since I couldn't figure out anything eloquent to say, I said the first thing that came to my mind. "I don't know, Liz. Just pray. Why don't you pray and ask God to reveal to you what's going on on the inside of you, and I'm sure He'll give you the answer. You're His favorite child, remember?" I said.

Liz smiled at me and took another bite of her muffin.

# Chapter 33

*In Search of Answers*

Liz came home to an empty house and headed straight for her bedroom. She wondered where her mom and baby brother were, but figured they must have gone grocery shopping as is their custom after attending the church's first service at eight o'clock.

Liz sat at the edge of her bed and grabbed her big Bible from the nightstand. She turned to the same scripture the guest minister had preached on this morning, which was Mark 11:24-25. She remembered hearing the preacher preach about this scripture in service and she had even stood up with the rest of the congregation. At that time she'd thought about who she needed to forgive, and no one had come to her mind. So she'd just prayed in the Spirit and prayed for the rest of the congregation that they would walk in forgiveness with whoever had hurt or wronged them.

Even though she had seen and read this scripture a million times and even though she'd paid it barely any mind this morning, for some reason Mark 11:25 seemingly jumped off the page. *And when ye stand praying, forgive, if ye have ought against any, that your Father also which is in heaven may forgive you your trespasses.*

The words *if ye have ought against any* kept playing over and over in her mind like a broken tape recorder. Liz closed her eyes, prayed in the Spirit and kept seeing those same words flash over and over in her mind and pierce her soul. "What is it, Father, God?" Liz asked her Heavenly Father. "Or who is it? Who do I need to forgive?"

Liz wasn't sure who it could be, but she knew it was someone. Somehow she knew that this person she needed to forgive, whoever it was, held the key to her future success in life and in relationships. She tried to think of someone to come to her mind; she tried to paint a picture of who it might be. But no one came. All she saw was blackness. She had no idea who this was that was causing her spirit to grieve.

Suddenly another scripture was brought to her remembrance seemingly out of the blue. Psalm 27:10 was whispered to her spirit as she ferociously flipped the pages of her Bible to find the words of that passage of Scripture. And it read, *When my father and my mother forsake me, then the Lord will take me up.*

And there it was—in plain black and white. The Lord had revealed to Liz the very person she needed to forgive.

The very person she couldn't visualize in her mind because she had never even seen him before.

It was her father.

After reading that scripture, Liz began to cry. She cried because she'd had no idea that never knowing her father, never being able to be referred to as "daddy's little girl" or never attending father/daughter functions together would cause such a deep hole of resentment to be placed in the pit of her heart—a hole that she'd had no idea was even there. And until that hole was replaced with the sea of forgiveness, God showed her that none of her relationships with men would ever be successful.

"Lord, what am I gonna do?" Liz cried out to her God. No response. "I want to forgive him, but I just can't! I can't, God, I can't!" Still no response. Liz thought about how her father abandoned her mother and left her all alone to raise Liz by herself. Liz wondered if her father even knew her first name, let alone what she looked like. Did he even know that his child with Pauletta Coleman twenty-eight years ago was a girl?

Liz couldn't see forgiving someone so selfish and so absent from her life. Someone who probably didn't even care. She wished she could get some type of an explanation from him as to why he'd just up and left. *Was he afraid to face the responsibility of being a dad? Did he really hate Mom that much that he purposely left her high and dry? When Mom used to tell me about Dad, how he was just a no-good, lazy drunk and a crazy supplier of sperm, was she really telling the truth?*

Liz heard the front door shut as Ms. Coleman entered with bags of groceries in one hand and baby Joshua on her hip.

"Liz, girl, come help me with these groceries, will you!" Ms. Coleman yelled.

Liz wiped her tears and attempted to recompose herself as she went to the front room and immediately grabbed baby Joshua from out of Ms. Coleman's arms.

"I said grab the groceries, not the baby, girl!"

"I know," Liz said. "I just wanted to tell my little man good afternoon. Good afternoon, little man!" Liz planted a wet one on Joshua's cheek, then blew on it, causing the baby to laugh out loud.

"He loves when I do that, ya know," Liz told Ms. Coleman.

"Yes, I do know," Ms. Coleman said as she gathered the groceries and placed them on the counter in the kitchen. "I know what my little man likes!" she added with a grin.

"Mom," Liz said in all seriousness.

"Yes, sweetie."

Liz wasn't quite sure how to proceed, especially since the last time she asked her mom about her father was back in her B.C. days. Maybe Ms. Coleman would be a little more understanding this time.

"Why did Dad leave?"

"What did you say?" Ms. Coleman asked.

Liz asked more slowly this time. "I said, why did Dad leave?"

"Where did that come from?" Ms. Coleman asked while unloading groceries.

"I mean, I know you said he left you at the altar and that he left you for another woman, but did he ever tell you why he ran away—from his child?"

Ms. Coleman just looked at her firstborn. "Well, if you

put it that way, no, he didn't. I mean, I don't exactly know *why* he did it, all I know is he left me and he knew I was pregnant. So by his actions I just concluded he didn't give a—I mean, he didn't care about me or you."

Liz bit her upper lip. She wasn't sure what to make of it. "Did you ever tell him I was a girl?"

"No, Liz!" Ms. Coleman yelled. "Where is all this coming from? I haven't talked to that joker since he left me twenty-eight years ago! No visits, no phone calls, no nothing! So, no, he has no idea you're a girl. You would think if he wanted to know, he would ask, right?"

Liz saw her mother was getting disturbed with the conversation so she placed baby Joshua back in Ms. Coleman's arms and retreated to her room, leaving Ms. Coleman speechless.

Once inside, Liz plopped back on her bed and held her hands. Her mother's response wasn't what she'd been exactly looking for, but it was what she'd expected. Ms. Coleman still hadn't healed from the pain he had caused her. *No answers found there,* Liz thought.

Just then she figured the only way she was going to find any true answers was that she needed to get it straight from the horse's mouth.

It was time for her to put a face to the man who'd helped bring her into this world twenty-eight years ago.

It was time for her to find her father.

# Chapter 34

*Choices*

Michelle tried reaching Sandy on her cell phone three more times after she left Starbucks with Liz.

"Sandy, this is Michelle. Give me a call, girl. It's important," Michelle said on Sandy's voice mail after calling her the fourth time. Michelle was starting to get worried. Or maybe Sandy was just ignoring her and no longer wanted to be her friend anymore.

Michelle pulled up into Sandy's driveway after deciding to drop by and see if she was home. When she saw Sandy's Neon wasn't parked out front, she figured she would pay Madear a visit.

*Knock, knock, knock.*

"Who is it?" Madear yelled from inside.

"It's me—Michelle!"

Madear unlocked all the locks on the door, opened it, then threw her full brown arms around Michelle's neck.

"Oh, Michelle! I'm so glad you're here! You're an answer to prayer!"

"Why, what's wrong?" Michelle asked.

Madear led Michelle inside to have a seat and brought her a glass of ice water.

"It's Sandy," Madear said.

"What about Sandy?"

"You mean you haven't talked to her?" Madear asked.

"No, I haven't talked to her since the party. Why, what happened?"

"I tried to knock some sense into that girl by telling her how wrong she was for messing around with that— what's his name?"

"Pierre."

"Pierre—yeah, him. And next thing you know that little fass thang done run out of here right after we talked and went back over his house at around two in the morning."

*At around two in the morning? Over his house? Again?* Michelle thought. She was fuming inside. *Maybe Sandy doesn't regret what she did, anyway. Maybe she wants to be with him. But how could she do this to me?*

"Yes. Again," Madear said, "I caught her about to sneak out of here so early in the morning. When I asked her where she was going, she wouldn't tell me. I figured she was going over that man's house again. So I tol' her, I says, 'Sandy, if you leave this house, you betta not come back here!' Do you know that girl walked right out the door? And when I come back from church this morning—'cause you know I had to go to God's house and pray for that chile—I come back, goes in her room and all of her stuff is gone!"

"Gone?" Michelle yelled. "You mean she moved out?"

"Gone! All her clothes and stuff is gone! She probably went to go be with that man—"

"I'm out, Madear, I gotta go," Michelle said. She left the glass of water on the coffee table and headed toward the front door.

"Where are you going?" Madear asked.

"I just gotta go somewhere and figure some things out. I'll let you know what happens, okay, Madear?"

"Okay. Well I wish the best of luck to you," Madear said as Michelle closed the door. "I hope you able to knock some sense into that child's head, 'cause I sure wasn't!"

Michelle got in the car and phoned her friend.

"Liz, what you doing?"

"Just sitting in my room thinking about some things. Why? What's going on? You sound all excited."

"Girl, Sandy just moved out of Madear's!"

"What? Moved out? Where did she go? That girl ain't got no money!"

"I got a feeling she went to live with Pierre."

"Pierre!"

"I wouldn't be surprised. You know how he can manipulate and worm his way into getting whatever he wants."

"You do have a point there. But my question is, what does this have to do with you?"

"What do you mean, what does it have to do with me? Sandy's my friend! She's my sister in Christ! I can't leave her hanging!"

"Hmph. Some friend. A friend who fools around with her friend's boyfriend."

"Ex-boyfriend, Liz."

"Whatever. So what are you about to do, go rescue her again?" Liz said in reference to the last time they'd rescued Sandy from a man—the one who'd sexually assaulted her almost two years ago.

"Liz, now, you know you ain't right for that one."

"But, Michelle, I think I am right. Why don't you come over here and we can pray and supplicate for her. Just running over there to try and rescue her won't work if she doesn't want to be rescued. You gotta remember that it's not all Pierre's fault. Sure, he may be the one opening the doors of his home, but nobody told her to take him up on his offer and go live with him."

"But, Liz," Michelle pleaded, "Sandy doesn't know what she's doing! She's still young in the Lord. She still needs us to tell her the truth!"

"Young in the Lord? That girl been at Hype for Jesus Church long enough to know right from wrong. It's her choice if she wants to ruin her life by putting herself in compromising situations where she can be taken advantage of. All I gotta say is, you've given her her wings, now it's time for you to let Miss Sandra Moore fly, Michelle. The Word says you have before you life and death. We have a choice to make. And apparently she has chosen the route she wants to take."

"But, Liz, we can't just leave her! God didn't leave us! When we messed up over and over again, He didn't just give up on us, so why should we give up on Sandy?"

"But, Michelle, you forgot one thing—we're not God. Maybe it's time for us to allow her to depend on God more than us."

"Okay, Liz, you have a point. But can we help her out this one last time? Can you do this, Liz, for me? Please?"

Liz held the phone and finally replied, "Oh, all right."

"Yes!" Michelle said as she headed to Liz's house.

"But this is the last time—"

"I know, I know. Thanks so much, Liz! I'll see you in about ten minutes."

*Ding-dong.*

Michelle decided to ring Pierre's doorbell rather than bang on the door like a police raid. She and Liz had spotted both Sandy's Neon and Pierre's new Escalade in the driveway.

"Are you sure we're doing the right thing?" Liz asked Michelle as they patiently waited for a response. "I mean, I can't believe we're over here—"

"Who is it?" a male voice yelled from inside. Instead of replying, Michelle rang the doorbell again. Michelle spotted a single eye looking through the peephole.

"Michelle? Is that you? What are you doing here?" Pierre asked.

"Um, I wanna talk," Michelle replied, trying to use one of his famous lines.

Pierre opened the door, and Michelle and Liz immediately noticed he had nothing on but light blue shorts. Michelle had forgotten how perfectly cut he was. He looked as if he had been working out lately; his six-pack defined through his chocolate-brown skin, and his hairy legs were as lean as a horse's.

"Hey, Michelle," Pierre said and looked her up and down. "Liz," he added with a nod in Liz's direction. "What brings you two lovely ladies my way?"

"Um, may we come inside?" Michelle asked as sweet as Kool-Aid even though she knew Sandy was inside.

"Sure, come inside," Pierre said, then let them in. "I didn't mean to be rude. Excuse the mess—I haven't had a chance to clean up yet. I been kinda busy, ya know."

"Yeah, I bet," Liz said underneath her breath with folded arms. "Got anything to eat?" Liz asked and helped herself to opening the refrigerator door.

"Here, let me get that for you," Pierre said, then leaned over inside the refrigerator, and Michelle couldn't help but notice his perfect backside. *Lord, help me,* Michelle thought.

Pierre retrieved a glass pitcher of lemonade from the fridge and placed it on the gray marble kitchen counter as Liz and Michelle took a seat on the leather couch.

"You really have the place looking nice here," Michelle said, still wondering about Sandy's whereabouts.

"Thanks. A lot has changed since we were together," Pierre replied. Michelle wasn't sure if he was referring to his interior decorating or his newly found love interest.

"I see," Michelle said.

Pierre placed two glasses of lemonade on the glass coffee table in front of Michelle and Liz, then took a seat in the adjacent black leather chair, folding one leg across the other, revealing his manicured feet.

"Now tell me, how is it that I received the honor and privilege of two women of God visiting my doorstep today? Is the street team from the church out witnessing? Was I the next house on the list?" Pierre asked with a charming smile, then took a sip of ice water.

Michelle gave a fake laugh, scooted to the edge of the couch and said, "No, not really. Liz and I were in the neighborhood and we just thought we'd stop by."

Pierre gave Michelle an accusing glare.

"Okay, well, maybe that's not the *only* reason I stopped by. I came by to check on Sandy. Is she here?" Michelle looked around the room.

"Sandy? Sandy—oh, she's here, all right," Pierre assured them.

After a brief pause Liz asked, "Well, where is she?"

"Sandy, baby, come out here! You have a couple visitors!" Pierre yelled toward the back room.

*Did he just call her "baby"?* Michelle thought.

Sandy came out from the bedroom in an extrashort pink satin lingerie slip with white lace barely covering her small breasts. She took five steps to the front, then was startled as she saw Michelle and Liz looking at her with their mouths open wide.

"Hi, Sandy!" Liz greeted her with a wide smile.

"Hi, Liz. Hi, Michelle," Sandy said sheepishly. "What are you two—"

"Oh, we were just in the neighborhood and just decided to drop by," Liz said in an extracheerful tone. "Oops, Sandy, dear, looks like you dropped something." Liz pointed to an imaginary item on the floor. "Wait a minute, you may not want to pick it up because if you bend over, your gluteus maximus might hang all out. That's assuming you're wearing underwear, which more than likely you're not—"

"Liz!" Michelle cut off her friend.

Sandy looked at the two of them, wondering what was really going on. "Did you come over here to make fun of me?" she asked. "Or did you come over here to damn me to hell?"

Michelle and Liz looked at each other.

Sandy waltzed over to where Pierre was sitting and placed her hand on his shoulder. "Well, if that's what you came here for, then fine. I'd rather burn in hell with my man than go through the rest of my life all alone!"

Michelle arose from her seat. "Sandy, you don't mean that. It's not even like that. Please forgive what Liz just said. You know how she can get sometimes. I was really coming over here to—to ask you to forgive me."

"Forgive you? For what?" Sandy asked with an attitude.

"For getting mad at you for hanging out with him," Michelle said while pointing at Pierre. "And for not calling you back."

"Oh, I see, you come here trying to be all nice and stuff asking for my forgiveness. But where were you when I needed you, Michelle Williamson? Where were you when Madear threw me out the house, huh? Oh, I forgot—you were somewhere praying or serving at the church or believing God for a breakthrough. You weren't anywhere thinking about me," Sandy said, then folded her arms.

Michelle couldn't believe Sandy's words. As much as she'd been there for that girl? As much as she'd come to her rescue? Michelle couldn't believe how Pierre could just sit through all of this with that stupid smirk on his face, as if he was *the man*.

"I'm here for you, baby," Pierre said, then grabbed Sandy by the waist and sat her on his lap. He then started to plant kisses on her bare arm.

"I know you are, Pierre, which is why I'm here with you now," Sandy replied and started rubbing his hairy leg.

Michelle felt as if she had to throw up. She tried to keep herself composed as the two lovebirds performed right in front of her as if she wasn't even there.

"Sandy, how can you sit there and say I haven't been there for you?" Michelle asked. "I've always been there for you! Remember Mark? Remember Carter? If *I* hadn't been there, no telling what would've happened to you!"

Pierre kept kissing Sandy's arm and suddenly gave Michelle a sinisterlike glare. His hand clutched Sandy's knee, then glided up her thigh. Sandy closed her eyes, threw her neck back and moaned in delight.

"Mmm. You're right, Michelle," Sandy cooed. "If you hadn't been there, no telling where I would be. You've always been there for me, like my guardian angel. But I've got a new angel now," she said, then smiled back at Pierre, who darted his eyes from staring at Michelle to back to Sandy.

Suddenly Liz shot up like a cannon and proclaimed, "Trick, you wouldn't have known who this joker was if he hadn't been Michelle's man before he was yours! I can't take any more of this foolishness. Michelle, girl, let's go! I'm about to lose my religion up in here, these folks is driving me crazy!"

"No!" Michelle yelled with desperation in her voice as she got in Sandy's face. "Sandy, girl, you're coming with me! You're either going to stay with me or you're going back to Madear's! But I am *not* leaving you here with Pierre!"

"Don't worry, Michelle. You had your chance," Pierre said. "Sandy's in good hands now—mine."

Sandy turned to face him again and kissed his lips.

Liz grabbed Michelle's arm, "C'mon, girl, let's go. We can tell when we're not wanted. Let's let them do their thang. God'll take care of them."

Liz led Michelle to the doorway, while Michelle kept looking back at the two of them kissing in the chair. As Liz opened the door to leave, Michelle looked one last time and saw Pierre pick Sandy up in his arms and lead her to his bedroom.

At Liz's urging, Michelle left his house and stood like a statue on the porch. "Liz, we gotta go back in there. I can't let her just—"

"Michelle, there's nothing else we can do," Liz said. "She has made her choice. She knows what she's doing. All we can do at this point is pray for the girl."

"But she's blind! He's got her blinded, just like he had me before! She doesn't see? He doesn't care about *her!* He's just using her!"

"I know that and you know that, but Sandy's going to have to learn on her own," Liz said.

Liz grabbed Michelle by the waist and forced her down the porch steps.

# Chapter 35

*What's His Name?*

Liz was relieved once she finally made it inside her own house. "Mom, I'm home!" she yelled, then figured maybe she shouldn't have been so loud, especially if Joshua was sleeping in his crib. Then again, sometimes that child slept through anything.

Ms. Coleman came from her bedroom and tied her satin robe. "Hey, Liz, what happened to you? Joshua and I missed you at dinner tonight. I made your favorite—pot roast and potatoes."

"I know. I'm sorry I missed dinner." Liz plopped on the couch and turned on the TV. "Had a crazy day today."

"Why, what happened?" Ms. Coleman asked, then grabbed the leftover roast from the fridge and warmed it up in the stove.

Liz stared at the TV screen and replied, "Well, it appears little Miss Sandy has gone on and stolen Michelle's boyfriend—or ex-boyfriend or whatever you want to call him."

"Who, Pierre Dupree? That fine young man from church with them hazel eyes?"

"Yeah, I guess."

"How in the world did that happen? I thought Sandy and Michelle were good friends."

"I thought so, too. Apparently not anymore."

"Really?"

"Sandy moved in with him."

"No!"

"Yup. Michelle and I just left from going over there to get her. Let's just say that plan didn't work. Sandy didn't want to leave."

"Well I'll be doggone. You know, Satan is busy, I tell you. He's got these young girls' minds all twisted. And here she is losing a great friendship over a man. That's one thing you should never want to do. It's not even worth it."

"I know," Liz agreed as she flipped through channels with the remote.

"And what about your man, Liz?" Ms. Coleman asked as she leaned her back against the kitchen counter and folded her arms. "I haven't heard you talking to him on the phone lately and I haven't seen him over here. What's going on with the two of you?"

Liz kept staring at the TV. "Nothing."

Ms. Coleman took a seat beside her daughter on the couch. "Oh, really? So you mean you can tell me what's going on in your friends' lives, but when it comes to your own, all you can say is 'nothing'?"

Liz set the remote down and faced her mom. "That's right, 'nothing.' Nothing is going on because nothing is there." After a slight pause Liz admitted, "We're not together anymore."

"What? What do you mean you're not together anymore? You broke up?"

"Yup. We broke up. Is the food ready?" Liz asked.

"What happened?"

"Nothing, Mom, dang!"

"Don't lie to me, girl. I know something happened. I knew something was wrong since you been walking around this house with a big frown on your face. So what'd you do, scare him off?"

Liz got up and shouted, "I don't want to talk about it, okay!"

Ms. Coleman looked up at her daughter, "Oh, no, you *didn't* just raise your voice at me."

Liz headed toward the kitchen. "I'm sorry, Mom. I didn't mean to yell. I just got a lot going on in my head, that's all. I didn't mean to take it out on you."

"That's okay, baby. I understand. I've known you for twenty-eight years, so I know that when you're ready to talk, you'll talk." Ms. Coleman started flipping channels on the TV.

"Mom?"

"Yes, hon."

"What's my father's full name?"

"Your father's full name? Why do you ask that?"

"Just wondering."

Ms. Coleman paused for a moment, looked at her daughter, then back at the TV and eventually said, "Ezekiel. Dominic Ezekiel Backhouse."

Liz hadn't known her father had a Biblical middle name.

"Everybody called him by his middle name. His friends used to call him Zeek. Zeek the Freak," Ms. Coleman added and laughed. "He used to play a mean basketball game back in his college days. I can remember when we first started going out. He was a senior in college and I was a senior in high school. Back then I was so proud to be going out with an 'older man.' All my friends were so jealous because he was the star player. All the ladies wanted him. They used to scream in the stands, 'Go, Zeeky! We love you, Zeeky!' But I used to just laugh on the inside as I heard them scream, because I knew after the game he was coming home to be with me."

"Y'all lived together?" Liz asked.

"Yup. We sure did. I lived with him while he finished college and I finished high school. Our parents didn't want us to be together because of the big age difference, so I left. It was like a true Romeo and Juliet story. We stayed in the basement on the east side of a two-family flat. The owner upstairs used to throw wild parties every Friday night. We used to be drinking and smoking up something crazy! Zeek and I would skip classes almost every Friday just so we could get high. Uh-huh, I remember those days. It was all good until he first used me as his punching bag when he came home drunk one night after losing a game."

Liz had forgotten how abusive her mom had said he was.

Ms. Coleman continued, "Thank God for saving me when He did. Maybe it was a hidden blessing that I didn't end up marrying that fool of a man. No tellin', he probably would've had me laid out dead somewhere."

Liz pondered her mother's words.

"Good ole Zeek the Freak," Ms. Coleman continued to reminisce. "He sure was a freak, though. He definitely earned the rights to his name."

"Please spare me the details, Mom," Liz said, then retreated to her bedroom.


Liz grabbed a seat in front of her computer and pulled up the Internet. "Welcome! You've got mail," the computer informed her.

"Thanks," Liz replied.

Liz Googled her father's name, Dominic Ezekiel Backhouse. Surprisingly she saw at least two articles with her father's full name. She clicked on the first one, which was a headline from a local newspaper: Dominic Ezekiel "Zeek" Backhouse named Detroit Mercer Community College's Most Valuable Player.

Once she clicked on the archived article, she was surprised to see a black-and-white photo of a tall, brown-skinned, lean man who was airborne about to slam-dunk a basketball. Liz's face drew closer to the computer as she tried to make out the man's features. Even though the photo was almost thirty years old, she saw how he resembled her. He had the same wide pug nose as she did. His eyes slanted slightly the same way hers did. His cheeks were full, just like hers, and his legs were long.

"So that's where I got my height from," Liz told the computer, considering she was five-eight and her mother was only five-one.

Liz couldn't believe she was staring at an old photo of her biological father—the man who'd helped bring her into this world.

Even though Liz had found a college photo of her father, she still wasn't satisfied. She wanted to learn more about this man who her mother had kept a secret from her for so long.

Liz clicked the back button on the computer and clicked on the second article: Spreading Holiday Cheer at Children's Hospital. The article was dated ten years ago, and the first sentence read, *Rufus Miller, Dominic "Zeek" Backhouse and Tyrone Lee Bailey sing a medley of Christmas songs to a standing-room-only crowd of children and parents at Children's Hospital.* The photo which accompanied the article showed a picture of three men, and the one who resembled Liz's father was leaning over, singing in a microphone to a little black girl with two ponytails, with a big, wide smile on his face. He was still tall and slim, had a thick mustache, chubby cheeks and the same nose.

*So this must be where I got my singing voice, because Lord knows Mom can't sing,* Liz thought.

Liz glared at the photo with envy. He appeared to be so full of joy while singing to some other little girl—some other little girl who probably knew of her own father's whereabouts, while this stranger sang to her while having a daughter of his own somewhere out there whom he'd decided to disown.

Liz looked harder at the picture and saw the shadows of two women smiling with glee and apparently clapping in the background. One woman was white, wearing a white jacket, and Liz figured she was a hospital worker. The other woman was black and appeared to be staring at Liz's dad in adoration. *Must be the other woman,* Liz thought.

Liz sat back in her chair and stared intensely at the photo with all kinds of emotions building up inside of her. *How could he?* she thought. *How could he look so happy and appear to be so nice, while my mom and I were home struggling to make ends meet? He didn't look to be lacking in anything. He was doing his "community service" for the holidays, "spreading holiday cheer," when he should've been spreading holiday cheer to me! I'm the one who was supposed to be his daughter!*

Anger boiled inside of her as tears stung her cheeks. Liz couldn't recall a single Christmas gift from her dad. Not a single birthday song performed especially for her from her father. The little girl in the photo got more time with him than Liz ever got in her own life. And, from the looks of it, he seemed to be pretty okay with it.

Liz couldn't understand. She secretly wanted to believe that her father was off somewhere being miserable and not out and about spreading joy to other people. What about his people? What about his family? Liz concluded she really didn't mean anything to him. It was as if he'd erased the fact that she ever existed.

Liz thought about shutting off the computer. She had had enough. She didn't care about finding him anymore or anything. She was mad. She was angry. She was hurt.

Just then, as if a small angel was seated on her shoulder, she heard a small voice whisper, *Find him.* She tried to shrug it off at first, as she wallowed in her own tears, but she kept hearing that same command over and over again, until it irritated her. "Okay!" she yelled out loud.

She Googled the words *find people,* and a list of possible selections came up. The one which caught her eye read, *Find people—find anyone. Phone number and address. Updated daily. Accurate. Free search.* She clicked on the link and was asked to enter information. She decided to do a name search since his full name was pretty uncommon.

She typed in his first name, middle initial, then last name. For the state she entered Michigan.

She hit the search button, then waited patiently as the prompt indicated, *Please wait as we search our database for Dominic E. Backhouse in Michigan.*

It seemed like eternity as Liz waited for the computer to bring up the results. What if there were none? What if he'd moved out of state? That last article was ten years old. She had no idea where he could be. She was sure her mother didn't know where and if he'd moved—the last time they had seen each other was over twenty-five years ago.

The computer finally brought up the results. It read, *We searched Dominic E. Backhouse and found zero records in Michigan.*

Liz hung her head low. Maybe her efforts were all in vain. She wouldn't be able to find him. It was nearly impossible.

After a few seconds of continued searching, a pop-up message from the search read, *We found zero results of Dominic E. Backhouse nationwide.*

Liz was ready to shut off her computer and call it a day. It was no use, she figured. She would never find her father.

After a few more seconds, another message popped up on the computer screen. *We found two records of Backhouse in Michigan.*

Could it be? Could it possibly be—a relative?

Liz clicked on the top name that came up on the search. Rhonda Backhouse. It listed her phone number and an address in Pontiac, Michigan. Liz grabbed her cell and called the number on the screen.

"Hello," a young man answered.

"Hello, may I speak to Rhonda Backhouse?" Liz asked. She couldn't believe she was doing this. Maybe she should just hang up right now.

"Hold on," the young man said, then yelled, "Mooooom!"

After a minute, a woman answered the phone. "Hello?"

"Hi, yes, is this Rhonda Backhouse?"

"Yes, it is. Who is this?"

Liz held the phone. Should she reveal her identity? Was this all a big mistake?

"Hello?" the woman asked again.

"Yes, I'm here," Liz said.

"Who am I speaking with?"

"Um, you're speaking to Liz. Liz Coleman."

"Liz Coleman?" the woman asked. "I don't know any Liz Coleman. I think you have the wrong—"

"Pauletta's daughter," Liz cut her off.

"Pauletta?" the woman asked. "Pauletta Coleman?"

"Yes," Liz assured her.

"From Becker High School?"

"Yes, from Becker." *How did you know the name of her high school?* Liz wondered.

"We went to high school together. She used to live with my brother," Rhonda said.

"Your brother? Would that, by any chance, be a Dominic Ezekiel Backhouse?" Liz asked with her hand shaking as she held the phone.

"Zeek! Yeah, that's my big brother. Now who is this?"

"This is Liz," Liz said again and held the phone, not believing she was speaking to a woman who could very well be her own flesh and blood, her very own aunt. "This is Zeek's daughter."

There was silence on the end.

"Zeek's daughter? I didn't know Pauletta had a child. Zeek got Pauletta pregnant?"

"Yes, he did, right before he left...us."

"Oh, Lord ha' mercy, Jesus," the woman said, then let go of the phone. All Liz could hear was the woman telling people in the background that Zeek's daughter was on the phone. Liz overheard people telling her it probably was a prank caller, but Rhonda assured them it wasn't since Liz told her Pauletta's name and high school.

"Hello!" an angry man answered the phone. "Who is this?"

"This is Liz," Liz said for the umpteenth time. "Who is this?"

"This is Earl Backhouse. You were just speaking to my sister. Now why you come calling here getting her all excited talking about you Zeek's child? Zeek didn't have any kids until he got married thirty years ago."

*So that means I could have siblings I don't know about,* Liz thought.

"I'm Zeek's child, sir. My mother, Pauletta Coleman, was pregnant with me when Zeek left Mama at the altar twenty-eight years ago. She had just found out she was pregnant, and when she told him, he left and never came back. She still went ahead and had me, so now I'm calling around trying to find out who he is, so I can meet him—for the first time."

"Well I'll be—" the man said in the phone. He yelled outside the phone, "Zeek done got Pauletta pregnant and done left her at the altar wit' a baby! I knew I shouldn't have believed him when he said the reason he didn't want to marry Pauletta was because of cold feet!" The man came back to the phone. "Sorry 'bout that, baby, we just in shock over here. You see, Zeek, since that day, done gone on and married another girl about a year after he and your mom broke up."

"So he's married now?" Liz asked. She'd figured that. "Is there any way you might have a phone number I can reach him?" Liz asked while biting her bottom lip.

"Rhonda, do you got Zeek's new phone number?" the man yelled.

"Huh?" Rhonda responded.

"Here, come grab the phone. She want Zeek's phone number."

"Hi, baby. You want Zeek's number?" Rhonda asked.

"Yes, please."

"You gotta pen?"

"I'm ready," Liz said with pen in hand.

"It's 248-555-1268."

"Okay, thanks. I'll try that number," Liz said.

"Elizabeth Coleman," Rhonda reflected out loud. "I can't believe this! You done made my day, girl! You know who you talking to? You talking to your aunt Rhonda! I have a niece! Well, glory be to the Lord!"

Liz smiled on the other end. She was glad at least her aunt Rhonda was glad to hear from her. And it sounded as though she had Jesus in her life. As for her father, Liz had no idea.

"Now after you speak to your father," Rhonda added, "you make sure you call me back. We're family, and the Backhouses stick together."

Liz wasn't sure about that last statement, especially since she wasn't quite a Backhouse. She was more like a Coleman, as Mr. Dominic "Zeek" Backhouse had refused to go through with the wedding ceremony.

Liz hung up the phone and wondered if "Zeek" would even want to hear from her at all.

Maybe he would deny that she was even his child. Maybe he would view her calling him as an interruption to his own apparently comfortable, cushy life. Maybe he would be upset that Liz put all of his business all out in the street by revealing her identity to his family.

*But it's my family, too,* Liz thought and concluded she might as well finish the deal and go ahead and call him.

She needed to know the other half of her life, which she had no clue about. She needed to know the other part of her own identity. She needed to know the source of her hurt—and her anger toward all men in general.

Liz hesitatingly dialed the number her aunt had supplied her with and waited as the phone rang three times.

A woman answered the phone on the fourth ring. "Hello?"

Liz thought she must have dialed the wrong number, as the woman who'd answered the phone sounded white.

"Hello?" the woman repeated.

"Hello," Liz said reluctantly. "Is there a Dominic Backhouse at this number? Uh, I mean Zeek Backhouse?"

"Zeek? There sure is. May I ask who's calling?" the woman asked politely.

*So he married a white woman?* Liz thought.

"Um, yes, this is Liz calling. Elizabeth Coleman... Zeek's daughter."

"I'm sorry, you must be mistaken. Zeek has two sons. He doesn't have any daughter."

"Um, yes, he does. I just spoke with my aunt Rhonda and uncle Earl. He has another daughter which he abandoned almost thirty years ago. My mom is Pauletta Coleman."

Liz heard silence on the other end for several minutes.

She couldn't hear anything in the background except for what sounded like a game on the TV.

"Hello?" Liz asked.

"I'm here." The woman sighed, then asked, "So you're Pauletta's daughter?"

"Yes, I am. And I'm also Zeek's daughter. They used to

go together while Zeek was in college and my mom was in high school."

"Yes, I know," the woman said, then added, "Can you come over for dinner tomorrow night? I'm sure he'd love to meet you in person."

Liz was definitely caught off guard with that invitation. She would've been content with just speaking to him on the phone—knowing he even existed. She had no idea she would be given an opportunity to meet him in person.

"Um, okay. I guess so. What's the address?" Liz asked, then jotted down the Pontiac address. She was surprised he still lived in Michigan.

"I'll see you tomorrow at five. I look forward to meeting you!" The woman almost sounded as if she was used to people announcing out of the blue that they were Zeek's child.

"Me, too," Liz said as the woman hung up the phone and Liz continued to hold the phone to her ear.

Liz was in utter shock as to what had just happened in the last thirty minutes. She'd found out she has an aunt and uncle who live less than forty-five minutes away from her; she'd found out she has a white stepmom; *and* she'd found out she has two half brothers she'd never even met before. More importantly, she had found her father.

# Chapter 36

*Effectual Prayer*

I sat on the couch with the Bible in my lap, staring into space. Even though Liz and I had just prayed for Sandy, I still couldn't rest knowing that right now Sandy and Pierre were probably having sex and I couldn't do a thing about it. I wondered if the motive behind my personal interest was out of sheer concern for Sandy's emotional well-being and spiritual growth or because I knew right now she was in between the sheets with a man I'd once loved and thought I would one day marry.

I slammed the Bible shut. I couldn't concentrate and couldn't quite find a scripture in the Bible about a friend sleeping with your ex and you being happy about it. I mean, I know I'm supposed to love my enemies, I know I'm supposed to forgive, but what about a hurting heart?

I know God will heal my broken heart, but what about these two people who I'd thought loved me, who I'll have to face every Sunday from now on at my own church?

Maybe I should switch churches?

Nah, I know God doesn't want to allow this situation to run me out of my own church home.

Liz was right—there is nothing else to do but pray.

Since I can't sleep and don't feel like fixing anything to eat, then I may as well keep praying.

I stood up and paced the living room floor and started praying fervently in the Spirit. As I prayed, I pumped my hands with such vigor and shut my eyes in an attempt to envision victory.

As I prayed in the Spirit, I placed Sandy's face in my mind. I saw her smiling, I saw her laughing, I saw her singing in the choir. I even saw the three of us at the restaurant after church, laughing at the table. I saw her in church, lifting her hands in worship to God. As I kept envisioning my friend, tears fell from my eyes. Even though I felt defeated, I kept praying and praying and praying for Sandy.

The enemy was not going to have her! The enemy was not going to keep her! She is my friend from high school and my spiritual assignment, and the devil was not going to take her away from me!

I prayed for an hour and a half straight, circling my front room so much that I probably wore out the carpet, but since I still didn't get a release to stop and still didn't have peace about the situation, I kept praying. I was so caught up in the spiritual realm that I thought I heard a light tap at the door.

After hearing the taps grow slightly louder, I realized that someone was at my door. Who could it be this late on a Sunday night?

I looked through the peephole and saw a woman with short, black, tousled hair facing the floor. I immediately opened the door and saw it was Sandy, with nothing but a coat on and pink stilettos with a broken heel.

I was so excited to see her that I gave her a huge bear hug. "Sandy!"

As I hugged her frail body, I almost felt as if she were going to break. I grabbed her and looked at her and saw she was still facing the floor, with her hair a mess.

I lifted her chin with my hand, which revealed teary eyes, smeared mascara and a red welt across her cheek.

"Sandy?" I asked. "What happened?"

I rushed her inside my place, shut the door, sat her on the couch and ran to the kitchen and ran cold water on a clean towel. I rushed back to sit beside Sandy and placed the dampened towel on her cheek.

"Sandy, what happened to you?" I asked.

Sandy didn't say a word.

"Did Pierre do this to you?" I had to ask.

Sandy kept quiet.

"Sandy, say something! Can you talk?"

"What do you want me to say?" Sandy finally said softly. "You were right?"

"You mean he tried to...rape you?" I asked, almost trembling myself. Maybe I should be calling the police.

"No, he didn't try to rape me," Sandy said.

"Well, what happened?"

After a slight pause Sandy said, "Well, when you and Liz left, he took me to his room and starting kissing me, then he laid me on his waterbed. He took off his shirt, laid his body on top of me, but then he started whispering in my ear and calling me...you."

"What?" I said.

Sandy continued, "All while he was kissing and feeling on me, he kept saying, 'Michelle, Michelle, you look so good, Michelle.' It was as if he was doing it on purpose or something, because he didn't even try to correct himself. So I got mad and eventually called him out on it."

I didn't know what else to say, so I asked, "Then what happened?"

"Then he got all mad at me all of a sudden, and we had a big argument. He really thought there was nothing wrong with calling out your name even though he was in bed with me. So we had a fight in the bedroom. I slapped him, and he slapped me back, so I grabbed my stuff and ran out the door. I broke my heel, too—shoot."

*So they got into a fight over me? Why did he keep calling my name? Did he secretly wish Sandy was me in the bed with him? Lord ha' mercy, Jesus.*

"I'm sorry, Michelle," Sandy said. "I'm sorry I tried to get in the way of you and Pierre. I know now that he really loves you and that he was probably just using me to make you mad."

I lowered my eyes. Maybe she was right. Maybe he does really love me.

"That's okay, Sandy," I said even though in my heart I felt it wasn't okay, especially for her to do what she did. I never want to lose a good friendship over any man—I don't care who it is. "You didn't know," I told her.

"But, Mickey, the bad part is, I wanted it," Sandy confessed.

"You wanted what?" I asked with an accusing glare.

After a slight pause Sandy said, "I wanted him to take me. I wanted him to have sex with me. I wanted him to make love to me."

I felt like a knife had just been stabbed in my back. After all this, Sandy still wished Pierre would have had sex with her?

"What's wrong with me?" Sandy said and then cried like a baby in her hands.

I placed my arm around her and rocked her from side to side. "Nothing's wrong, Sandy. You just made a mistake, that's all. Nobody's perfect."

"I know. But I can't even sin right."

I had to chuckle at that one. "Don't say that, Sandy. Why don't you take what happened as God's way of protecting you from sinning and from being hurt even more in the long run."

There was a slight pause as Sandy peeked up at me, then said, "You know, I didn't look at it that way."

"Yeah. I mean, a bruise will heal, but sometimes it takes a lot longer to heal a broken heart. So let's look at this whole experience as God's way of protecting you and keeping you from a broken heart."

Sandy sniffed and said, "You're right, Michelle." Sandy sat up on the couch. "You're always right. You always do everything right. I wish I could be like you."

"Don't say that," Michelle said. "God made us all unique in our own special way. There are a lot of things I like about you, Sandy."

"Like what?" Sandy asked.

"I like your spontaneity and the refreshing way you look at life, but, more importantly, I like the fact that you love God and have a heart for Him and are willing to confess your mistakes and your faults not just to Him but also to the ones you hurt. It was very big of you to come by here tonight and tell me what happened. Not many people would do that, Sandy."

"Really?" Sandy asked, wiping her tears.

"Nope."

"Well, the reason I came to you after what happened, Michelle," Sandy said as tears welled up in her eyes again, "is because you're all I got."

Sandy cried on my shoulder again, and I held her tight and kept rocking her from side to side, then kissed her head.

I was just happy to see her again and happy she'd come to me. To me, she was like the little sister I never had.

Nobody can ever tell me that my God doesn't hear and answer prayer. He hears it and He answers it—suddenly.

# Chapter 37

*Facing Fear*

Liz turned up her Donnie McClurkin while driving in her car. She played one of her favorite songs from his "Live in London" CD, "I'll Trust You," as she thought about the fact that she was on the way to meet her biological father for the first time.

She thought about how she really had to trust God, that He would lead and direct her as to the right words to say to this man whom she had never known. She wanted her father to know how she truly felt, but she didn't want to scare him off. She wondered how he would respond to seeing her for the first time? Would he welcome her with open arms? Would he be embarrassed by her? Would he be ashamed? Would he lie to his wife and say he'd never had any kids by any Pauletta Coleman?

As Liz parked on the street in front of a large yellow-brick two-story home in Pontiac, she saw that the address matched the one which she'd jotted as her father's address. She was ready to meet this man who most people call Dad. At least she could say she'd met him, if nothing else came of the whole thing.

Liz slowly walked up the walkway leading to her father's house while straightening her long black dress, which lightly blew in the wind. She hoped she was properly dressed for the occasion and that her father would accept her choice of attire. She hoped he wouldn't comment on her healthy size, since he was pretty slim in those photos online.

*Maybe he'll think I'm fat,* Liz thought. *Why do I even care?* Liz thought, then rang the doorbell. From the looks of the house and the matching silver Benzes in the driveway, Liz wondered if a maid was going to answer the door.

After several minutes, Liz heard no answer, so she rang the doorbell again.

*Maybe this was all a big mistake,* Liz thought, then turned around and headed back to her car.

Just then, the door opened and a woman called after her. "Liz?" she asked.

Liz turned around and saw a thin white woman with long blond hair who looked to be in her early forties. She wore a multicolored floral-print dress which complemented her tiny frame.

Liz smiled and headed back up the walkway.

"Hi, Liz, I'm Carolyn Backhouse—Zeek's wife," she said, then extended a hand and led Liz inside.

Liz walked inside and immediately noticed how beautiful the place looked. The living room was large, with cream, gold and black decor. The carpet was so soft and clean Liz wondered if she should take her shoes off at the door. A large movie-size flat-screen TV was in the front room, with an Xbox in front of it as if someone had been playing it just before she'd arrived. Just then, Liz remembered that she did have two half brothers.

Suddenly an extremely light-skinned young man with a curly afro came pouncing down the stairs sounding like a herd of elephants.

"Maxwell! How many times do I have to tell you not to run down the stairs?" Carolyn asked.

"Sorry, Mom," the teenager said and stood next to his mom, then stared at Liz. "So you're my sister?" the young boy asked.

Liz looked at the tall, lean young man who looked exactly like her father except for his complexion and hair texture.

"Max, let's not be rude," Carolyn said. "Max, meet Liz. Liz, meet Max. And from what I believe, you're right, Max—she *is* your sister."

"Sweet!" Max said, then shook Liz's hand vigorously. "I never knew I had a sister. Pleasure to meet you!"

"Pleasure to meet you, too," Liz said. She wondered if her other half brother was going to come down the stairs, too. She stared at the spiral staircase, but nothing happened. She didn't quite know what else to say to Carolyn and Max, but she did wonder where her father was and why *he* hadn't greeted her at the door.

Carolyn led the two of them to the dining room to be seated for dinner and then she disappeared from the room.

Liz, not quite sure of what to say exactly, just smiled at her half brother whom she'd just met. He smiled in return.

"So, um, what school do you attend?" Liz asked to break the silence.

"I go to Pontiac High!" he responded.

"Oh, um, are you involved in any extracurricular activities there?"

"Yup, I play basketball. I'm real good at it, too!"

*Nice,* Liz thought. *Basketball, just like my father. Or shall I say* our *father. Where is he, anyway?*

After several minutes of small talk, Carolyn returned to the dining room table and gave Liz a sheepish grin. "Dinner will be served in a moment," she said.

Carolyn retreated to the kitchen and returned with a bowl of tossed salad and family-style dishes of mashed potatoes, asparagus tips and a plate of smoked salmon. After placing the dishes on the table and taking a seat, Carolyn asked, "Would anyone like to say grace?"

Liz looked confused. "Where is my father?" she asked.

"Oh, he'll be joining us soon," Carolyn said, then added, "Max, would you like to lead us in blessing the food?"

Liz was fuming inside. "I am not going to eat anything until I see my father! Is he here?"

Max and Carolyn just looked at each other.

"Oh, yes, he's here," Carolyn assured her.

"Then where is he?" Liz demanded, then slammed the cloth napkin down on the table and arose from her seat.

"Like I said, he'll be here—"

"I don't want to hear that! Where is he? Where is he at?" Liz yelled, then stormed out of the dining room and rushed into the living room and yelled, "Zeek Backhouse, where are you?"

Carolyn followed after Liz and placed her hand on Liz's shoulder. "Now there's no need to get loud—"

"No need to get loud?" Liz said with an attitude, then shook Carolyn off her. "No need to get loud? The man I've never known for twenty-eight years of my life is still not showing himself to me? What are you, scared?" Liz yelled loud enough for Zeek to hear her if he was upstairs. "There is nothing worse than a scared black man! You coward!"

"Now, Liz," Carolyn said.

Maxwell entered the living room, then Liz dashed to the front door.

"Liz, wait!" Carolyn called after her. "Zeek!" she yelled upstairs. "Please!"

Liz struggled to open the front door, then heard Carolyn announce, "There he is!"

Liz looked up and saw a tall, lean, dark-skinned man with a pug nose, a pot belly and a receding hairline slowly make his way downstairs wearing black slacks, black dress shoes and a neatly pressed white-collared shirt. His eyes looked weary and worn out, as if he may have been crying.

Once he made it to the last step, he gave Liz a once-over, then headed to the front room, plopped on his long cream leather couch, then turned the TV to a game.

Liz was devastated.

"Is that all you're gonna do, just sit there?" Liz said, then inched her way to the living room and yelled behind his head, "You just gonna ignore me? Oh, I get it, you're here in Stonegate Pointe now, with your white wife, your nice home, your mixed kid and your cushy life. Well, what about me, *Daddy*? What about me?"

Carolyn stood holding her youngest son.

"Oh, I forgot—you're not my daddy," Liz said. "A daddy is there for his little girl. A daddy takes his little girl for walks in the park, shows his little girl how to ride a bike and fixes his little girl's new toys on Christmas day." Liz's voice started cracking as she yelled, "A daddy sticks up for his little girl and is his little girl's hero. Well, you know what, Mr. Backhouse, you're definitely no hero of mine."

Zeek turned the game up louder.

"Yeah, that's right. You go ahead and turn the TV up. Go ahead and try to block what I'm saying out of your mind, the same way you tried to act like I was never born. If it were up to you, I probably would have been aborted. So Mom was right. You remember my mom, don't you? Pauletta Coleman?" Liz said.

At this point Carolyn asked Maxwell to go upstairs and he obeyed.

"Remember her?" Liz continued. "Remember you were about to marry her, but you bailed out at the last minute once you found out she was pregnant with me? Remember you left her? You left us to fend for ourselves? Remember that?" Liz choked up even more, and Carolyn just stared at Liz, who kept staring at the back of her father's head.

"Well, I just wanted you to know I turned out okay, *Dad*," Liz said and wiped her nose. "I graduated from college. I was a teacher and now I'm in full-time ministry. Even though your sorry butt decided to ignore the fact that I was even born, I had a man to take care of me. A man who cared about the fact that I existed and cared about what I was going through. A man who raised me right and made sure I did the right thing. A man who was always by my side during those daddy/daughter recitals that I had to miss and who called me his daddy's little girl—and His name is Jesus, *Dad*. His name is Jesus!" Liz screamed. She felt as if she were talking to a brick wall.

With that, Zeek got up from the couch, left the room and headed toward the kitchen.

Liz wiped her eyes and said to Carolyn, "I'm sorry."

"You don't have to apologize," Carolyn said.

"No, I'm sorry. I'm really sorry. I'm sorry I came to your home. I'm sorry I interrupted your life. I'm sorry I even came here. Obviously he doesn't even care I exist."

"That's not true," Carolyn said. "He does care. Come here, have a seat."

Carolyn invited Liz to sit on the couch. "Liz," she began, "I want to apologize about what happened with your father. That was very rude, and I just want to say I'm sorry on his behalf."

Liz, with dry eyes now, looked Carolyn right in her crystal-blue eyes and said, "I know you mean well and I know that you're his wife and all, but please don't speak for him. He should be man enough to speak for himself. Oh, but I forgot—since he wasn't man enough to claim a child and help raise her financially, then of course I shouldn't expect him to be man enough to admit when he is wrong."

Carolyn looked down and said, "He's scared, Liz."

"Scared?" Liz asked. "What does he have to be scared about?"

Carolyn looked up at Liz. "He's scared because he doesn't know what to say or do now that you're here. He feels bad for not being in your life, so now he just doesn't know how to respond. But he does love you, though."

"Love?" Liz asked. "You call *that* love? That's not the kind of love I read about in the Bible."

"I know."

"Love doesn't just walk out on you! Love is giving. Love cares!"

"I know. And he *does* care. Trust me. When I told him I talked to you on the phone last night, he froze. He was scared. He was scared about what you would think of him. He wanted to meet you, but he was scared you wouldn't forgive him."

"Forgive him?" Liz asked.

Carolyn nodded her head.

"After he left me and my mom with nothing?"

"I know. Trust me, I know all about it."

Liz gave Carolyn an accusing glare. "What *do* you know?"

Carolyn shifted in her seat, then said, "I met your father while I was in high school."

"And?" Liz said.

"I attended Becker High with your mom."

Liz sat back on the couch and sighed.

"I remember when he left Pauletta at the altar. He told me about it right after it happened. That night, actually—he and I were friends."

"Friends, huh? So you the one who stole my mom's boyfriend."

"No, we were just friends at the time. He helped me with one of my science projects and he helped me in math. He was such a math whiz, and I was so horrible in it. He really came to my rescue," Carolyn said.

"I bet he did," Liz muttered.

"But we were never more than just friends, really."

Liz didn't believe her. She was sure this Carolyn lady had been making the moves on her dad while he'd so-called helped her with her homework. What would a grown man in college want anything to do with helping a high school girl, anyway? Only a fool would believe that nothing had gone on between the two of them.

"Okay, so you got together and hooked up after he left my mom," Liz said. "What does that have to do with me?"

"He told me about you back then," Carolyn said. "He told me about Pauletta being pregnant. And, to be honest, I actually told him he should have her get an abortion and I even offered to pay for it."

"What the?"

"I know, I know. That definitely wasn't right. Dear God knows I wouldn't wish that on anybody nowadays, but back then I was out for my own interests. I had a crush on your father all throughout my years in high school. I idolized him."

"I knew it! I knew you stole my father away from me!" Liz said and shot up from her seat. "All this talk about the two of you being 'just friends.' Yeah, right, you were just looking for a perfect opportunity to steal my father away from my mom! My mama used to always say you can never trust a white woman around your man."

"Now wait a minute, Liz," Carolyn said in anger.

"No, you wait a minute, Carolyn!" Liz said. "All this being supernice stuff and inviting me over to dinner at your house stuff. I know what you're up to. Like my father, you wish I was never born, either! If you had your way, I would have been killed before I was ever given a chance to live." Liz bent over and got in Carolyn's face. "Well, you know what? You may have gotten my father, but I'm still here. I'm alive and well, praise the Lord!" Liz said, then arose and said, "Now get me out of this crazy house!"

Liz headed to the door, then heard a male voice call her name. "Elizabeth!" The voice sounded so deep and authoritative she felt compelled to stop dead in her tracks.

Liz turned around and saw her father heading toward her.

"Liz, I'm sorry," he said. He choked up and extended his hand and repeated, "I'm sorry, Liz, for everything."

Liz just looked at her father's big hand the color of oil. The hand she wished she could recall holding hers as they'd walked at Metro Beach as father and daughter. The hand she wished she could remember stroking her hair or rubbing her back as a young child well into the night in order to keep the bogeymen away. The hand that should have given her a high five when she received an A on an essay paper. The hand that she wished would have caught her if she fell down or picked her up and told her, *I love you, baby girl.*

Zeek continued, "I'm sorry I wasn't there for you. I'm sorry I left Pauletta to raise you by herself." Zeek shook his head and grabbed it with the hand Liz refused to acknowledge. "If I had to do it all over again, Lord knows I would do it differently. Lord knows it wouldn't be the same."

Liz looked at her father, then thought about his last words. So maybe he did regret not being there for her. Maybe he did wish he'd been there during those special father/daughter moments just as much as she did. Maybe he did wish he could turn back the hands of time.

Liz knew she couldn't control the past, but the one thing she could control was the present. Even though her father abandoned her and her mom almost thirty years ago, he was there now, standing right in front of her, whereas the only image of a father baby Joshua would ever have would be old photographs of Richard before he'd gotten killed in the car accident.

The man who'd fathered Liz was standing before her, in the flesh—with her same nose, same eyes and same pitiful look on his face that she had when she knew she'd done wrong.

Liz looked up at her father and softly muttered, "I forgive you, Dad."

He extended his hand again, and Liz took it this time. He then grabbed Liz and gave her a big hug, and they cried real tears in each other's arms.

Shortly after, a thunderous noise came from the stairs again as footsteps made their way down once more. Maxwell returned, this time with another young man who was a foot taller than Max was, with skin the color of a sunset and short, curly brown hair.

Liz and her father let go of one another and looked at the two figures who stood in front of them.

"Liz, these are your brothers, Max and Malcolm," Zeek said and extended his hand toward them both.

"She's met Max," Carolyn said and walked back up to the front and stood next to Zeek.

"Carolyn, I'm sorry I—"

"That's okay, sweetheart. I understand," she said. "All is forgiven."

Liz felt relieved to hear her say that. After all those mean things she'd said to her, it was good to hear that Carolyn realized that she'd only said those things out of her own anger and hurt.

"It's a pleasure to meet you, Malcolm," Liz said, then extended her hand. She couldn't get over how handsome he was. He looked at Liz suspiciously at first, then looked over at his parents, not sure if he should accept her gesture.

"It's okay," Carolyn assured him.

"I won't bite," Liz said. "I turned my stingray powers off today. I may turn them back on tomorrow, though, so watch out."

Young Maxwell laughed, while Malcolm just looked at her and eventually shook her hand out of courtesy.

"You gotta firm grip there, Mr. Malcolm. You play any sports?" Liz asked.

"No, I don't play any sports," he muttered.

"Then what do you do?" Liz asked.

"I sing," Malcolm said.

"Malcolm is the lead singer in a rock band," Zeek said while holding on to Carolyn's waist.

Liz looked back over at Malcolm and said, "Oh, really. Is that so?"

"Yeah," Malcolm said, then scratched his head.

Liz could tell he was really shy. She couldn't picture him singing lead in any rock band. Then again, some people say you change into a different person when you perform on stage.

"I sing, too," Liz said, then looked back at her father, who apparently had passed his singing ability down to two of his offspring.

"Oh, yeah?" Malcolm asked with interest. "What do you sing?"

"Mainly gospel. I mainly sing for the Lord. I guess I have to, being an Evangelist and all."

"You're an Evangelist?" Malcolm asked with brightened eyes.

"I sure am," Liz said.

Maxwell asked, "So you're like those preachers on TV?"

"Something like that," she said. "But it's all good. I love what I do. I love spreading God's message to His people. Do you boys know about God's message?"

"Yeah, we know, we know about God's message, isn't

that right boys?" Zeek said while giving his wife a squeeze on her side.

Max nodded his head, while his older brother Malcolm kept looking downward.

"Well, amen, I'm sure you do. But can we just pray since we're all here together?" Liz asked. "Lord knows when and if we'll ever have this opportunity again."

Zeek and his wife drew closer and all of them made a small circle, held hands and closed their eyes.

After the prayer, Liz was fighting to hold back tears. She didn't want her father to think she was a big baby, even though right about now she was overcome with emotion. She felt as if she were having an out-of-body experience. As if she were starring in a dream. Meeting her father for the first time *was* a dream. It was a dream come true.

Zeek took one last look at his daughter, smiled at her and said, "Thank you, Elizabeth Coleman. Thank you for changing my life." And he grabbed her once again for one last hug for the day. It was a hug that somehow made up for the twenty-eight years that she'd gone without feeling the warmth and sincerity of a biological father's embrace.

Liz made it back home and plopped her car keys on the kitchen counter.

"So how'd it go?" Ms. Coleman turned around and asked from the couch. Liz remembered that her mother had been sitting on the couch when she'd left to meet him two hours ago. Had she been waiting for Liz to return home the whole time?

Liz grabbed a can of orange Faygo pop out the fridge and poured it in a glass. "It went okay, I guess."

"You guess? What happened?" Ms. Coleman turned around and asked her. "Was he even there?"

"He was there. We met, that's all." Liz didn't feel like going into detail with her mom, who was obviously still bitter about the whole thing.

"Oh. Did you meet his wife?"

Liz sat in the love seat next to her mom. "I sure did," Liz said, hoping Ms. Coleman wouldn't ask her to reveal her identity.

"Was she nice?"

"She seemed to be pretty nice, I guess."

"Do I know her?" Ms. Coleman asked.

"What do you mean, do you know her?" Liz wondered if she'd suspected something the whole time they'd been in high school.

"Did I know the woman? I mean his wife. What's her name?"

"Her name is Carolyn."

"I knew it, I knew it!" Ms. Coleman proclaimed.

"What, Mom?"

"Carolyn Hunter. I knew that tramp had her eyes set on Zeek. I knew it! Every time Zeek would come up to my school to visit me, she always seem to be around, all smiling and carrying on. She was a cheerleader, you know. She used to bounce around giggling all in his face every time he visited our school. I *knew* it!"

"Oh, well, you were right then. They live in Stonegate

Pointe in Pontiac and they have two sons. Or shall I say I have two half brothers."

"Did you meet 'em?" Ms. Coleman asked.

"Yeah, I met them. It took a while for the older one to come downstairs, though, but he finally did and he seems to be pretty cool…"

"It prob'ly took him a while to come down because he's probably older than you," Ms. Coleman said.

"Huh?" Liz asked. She'd thought he was in his early to mid twenties, not late twenties or early thirties. She must have been wrong.

"There were rumors that Zeek got Carolyn pregnant around the same time I was pregnant with you," Ms. Coleman said. "The rumor also was he left me at the altar because as soon as I told him I was pregnant, Carolyn told him she was pregnant, too. So he chose to go with her over me."

"Dang."

Liz looked over at her mom, who reached inside the pocket of her satin robe and pulled out a pack of cigarettes.

"I'm sorry, Mom," Liz said, then noticed the pack of cigarettes and proclaimed, "Mom! I know you're not about to smoke again? You quit over a year ago!"

"Why not?" Ms. Coleman added with a swear word, "I need something to calm my nerves right about now."

"C'mon, Mom, you don't need this!" Liz said, then snatched the pack of cigarettes from her hand. "All you need is God. C'mon, Mom, let's pray."

"I don't want to pray!" Ms. Coleman said.

"Evangelist Coleman, I suggest you join me in a word of prayer."

Ms. Coleman obliged and bowed her head as Liz grabbed her hands. "Father, God, in the name of Jesus, I thank You because You are sovereign and magnificent. I thank You that You have been a mother for the motherless and a father for the fatherless. I thank You that You have empowered my mother, Pauletta Coleman, to raise me right, in that I am now living a life in order to serve and please You. I pray for Your strength right now, for both of us, that You would keep us in Your perfect peace. That You would help us to walk in love with Your people and give us a heart to forgive those who have done us wrong or who have broken our hearts. We pray that You give us the courage to move on, forgetting those things from the past and reaching toward the mark of the prize of the high calling in Christ Jesus. We look to You, Lord, knowing You hold the key to our destinies. And we thank You for those trials and tribulations we have gone through, by counting them all joy. In Jesus' name we pray, amen."

"Amen," Ms. Coleman muttered through watery eyes. She arose, tied her satin robe, then headed to the nursery room to check on Joshua.

Before she left the room she turned around and said, "Thanks, Liz. Oh—and, Liz, you gotta message on the machine. Some lady from a church wants you to speak at their conference. Prophetess Parker or something like that. You may want to give her a call back."

"Okay, Mom. Thanks," Liz said, then arose and pressed

Play on the answering machine in the hallway next to the bathroom, listened to the message and retrieved the number of the woman calling from Victory in Jesus Church in Highland Park, Michigan.

Liz looked at her watch and saw that it was almost eight o'clock, which may not be too late to return the woman at the church's phone call.

Liz dialed the number on the house phone.

"Hello," an older woman answered.

"Hello, may I speak to Prophetess Clara Parker?"

"This is Prophetess Clara Parker."

"Hi. My name is Elizabeth Coleman. I'm returning your phone call."

"Yes. Hi, Elizabeth Coleman! How are you?"

"I'm fine."

"Thanks for getting back with me so soon. My niece heard you speak to the young women at the ladies' shelter before, so I thought it might be a good idea for you to speak at my church's upcoming singles' conference."

*Oh, great,* Liz thought. *I get to speak at a singles' conference.* Liz had never spoken at a singles' conference before. She mainly spoke to women exclusively, but based on the number of men who attend church regularly, Liz figured it might still be her ministering to a bunch of women.

"Okay. When is it?" Liz asked.

"It's this Thursday night. I know it's last-minute—the person who was originally supposed to speak had to cancel."

*This Thursday,* Liz thought. *That only gives me three days to prepare a sermon. Well, it's not like I'm working right now, so I may as well take any speaking engagement I can get.*

"Is there a certain topic or anything?"

"Oh, not really," Prophetess Parker said. "Just an encouraging word to the singles. Whatever the Lord lays on your heart."

"Oh, okay."

"Do you charge?" Prophetess Parker asked.

"I'm sorry?" Liz asked.

"What's your honorarium fee?" the prophetess asked.

Liz hadn't quite gotten around to figuring out her honorarium fee yet. She wasn't quite sure what to charge, if anything.

"Oh, well, um, I'm not sure. A love offering should be fine," Liz said, then regretted her last words. She hoped her request for a "love offering" would at least cover the gas it would take to get to that side of town.

Liz wondered how people survived financially by ministering full-time. It's all for the Lord, she knew, but a person's gotta eat.

"Oh, well, I'll have the church take up an offering for you at the end of the program."

Liz's eyes brightened up. She thought about how if there were at least one hundred people and they all gave a dollar, that would at least be one hundred dollars.

"Thanks!" Liz said.

"Oh," Prophetess Parker continued, "and we'll have to split the offering between you and the other two speakers that night."

*Just great,* Liz thought. *So that means I'll be going home with less than thirty-five dollars.*

"That's fine," Liz said. "Can you e-mail me the information about the event? The location, time and stuff like that?"

"Sure thing, baby," Prophetess Parker said. "I'll have my niece e-mail you. You know I'm not too hip on all this computer stuff, but she can do it."

"Okay, Prophetess Parker," Liz said. "Thank you so much for inviting me! We're going to have a blessed time in the Lord."

"Oh, I'm sure we will, Minister Coleman. I have heard some great things about you. Thanks for accepting the invitation! My niece, Candice, said you were real good. She said you really blessed her the last time she heard you speak."

"Thanks," Liz said, then hung up the phone and smiled. Even though, starting out, she may not command top dollar, just knowing she had enriched someone else's life in some way was motivation enough for her to move forward in the calling that God had for her life.

# Chapter 38

*Let It Go*

Liz prayed quietly in the waiting room at Victory in Jesus Church in order to prepare for her upcoming sermon. She had entered through the back door and wasn't sure how many people were there at the medium-size church building, but she believed that God had given her a Word especially for the single people she was about to minister to. She prayed and asked God to cast out the nervousness she felt inside, as Prophetess Parker entered the room wearing a navy-blue skirt suit and matching hat with silver beads and asked Liz to prepare to enter the pulpit.

As Liz got closer to her destination, she heard claps and was ushered out onto the pulpit with a smile by Prophetess Parker. Liz stood in front of the pulpit and noticed a packed house of almost two hundred people—mainly women and a third men—staring back at her. She was so nervous and didn't quite know what to say, but she opened her mouth to speak anyway.

"Well, praise the Lord, saints," she said as she grabbed the microphone from off the stand and placed her Bible and notes on the clear pulpit.

"Praise the Lord!" the lively congregation responded in unison.

"Well, it sounds like you all are alive and well this evening," Liz said. "You're looking sharp."

Some members of the congregation chuckled.

Liz was glad she'd decided to wear her black two-piece skirt suit with a silver brooch. She wasn't overdressed but not underdressed either. She figured one could never go wrong with black.

Liz opened her Bible to her main text, then said, "Okay, before I get started, I want to go before the Lord in prayer. Can you all please bow your heads with me." Everyone obliged.

"Heavenly Father, I come to You in the name of Jesus. I ask that You speak through me, to speak a word in due season to Your people. Not my will, but Thy will be done. In Jesus' name, amen!"

"Amen!" the church responded.

Just then, Liz spotted Michelle and Sandy grabbing two empty seats in the third row. Liz smiled at them, then began.

"Glory to God. Well, first of all I'd like to thank Prophetess Clara Parker for inviting me out tonight. What a blessing!"

Prophetess Parker smiled from her chair on the back of

the stage. The first speaker, Evangelist Marie Lane, was seated next to her, and there were two empty seats for Liz and the final speaker.

"You know, when Prophetess Parker asked me to minister to the singles today, I really didn't know what to minister about. She asked me to minister about whatever I felt the Lord laid on my heart, so I really believe the Word I have for you all this evening is definitely a Word from God."

"All right!" someone yelled from the congregation.

"Turn with me, if you will, to Philippians 3:13. When you get there, say 'Amen.'" Liz heard rustles from Bibles, then voices saying, "Amen."

She then said, "If you're not there yet, say 'Oh, me.'" Members of the congregation laughed.

"Okay. Philippians 3:13. And it reads, *Brethren, I count not myself to have apprehended, but this one thing I do, forgetting those things which are behind and reaching forth unto those things which are before.*"

Liz stepped away from the pulpit and spoke directly to the audience. "The title of today's message is 'Forget the past and move on.'"

"Amen, Evangelist!" someone said from the congregation.

"I said, forget the past and move on," Liz repeated.

"Well," someone said from the fifth row.

Liz continued, "You see, as singles, a lot of us have made mistakes in our past. We've done some wrong things in our past. We've made mistakes when it comes to relationships. But God wants us to forget the past and move on!"

"Hallelujah!" a woman shouted from the front row.

"God wants to heal us from our past. He wants to deliver us from our past. He wants us to be healed so that we can be whole when He is ready to present to us the mate that He has for us."

"I know that's right!" a lady said from the far right.

"He wants us to walk in love and He wants us to forgive those who have hurt us in the past."

"Amen!" a man said from the second row.

Liz stepped up closer to the audience. "Now, I don't usually do this. I don't usually put my business out on the streets like this."

"Make it plain," someone said.

"Those who really know me, like my two friends here supporting me in the third row, know that I'm a pretty reserved and quiet individual. But I feel the Lord wants me to share this with you so that it may help someone else."

"Take your time," an older gentleman said.

"You see, I just recently met my father—for the first time."

"Well," someone said.

"Here I am, a grown woman, knocking on thirty, and one day the Lord laid it on my heart to try and find my father. And I found him through the Internet."

"All right," a man said from the front.

"I found him, I called and spoke to some relatives on his side that I never knew and, not long ago, I met him at his house—him and his wife and two sons."

"Lord ha' mercy," a lady wearing a church hat said from the second row.

"And, to be honest, when I met him, I was mad!" Liz shouted.

"Keep it real," a young woman said from the fifth row.

"I was angry!" Liz said with an angered look on her face. "At the time I thought to myself, how can he live like this, with this family over here," Liz said, pointing to the left, "and *deny* the fact that he has a whole 'nother family over there, with no financial support, no emotional support, not even a birthday card on my birthday!" Liz said, pointing to the other side.

"You betta preach!" a young woman shouted from the left side of the congregation.

"God really had to deal with me on that thang. But you know what I found out after taking it to the Lord in prayer?"

"What's that?" someone asked out loud from the congregation.

"I found out that the anger I held inside for my father, for leaving me and my mother cold, and the hurt I felt inside, which came from believing he wanted to have nothing to do with me, was affecting my relationships with men."

"Lord ha' mercy, Jesus," an older woman said from the front row.

"I didn't trust men," Liz admitted to the congregation. "I didn't believe men. I couldn't believe that any man besides God could ever really love me for who I was, because I never knew the love of my own biological father." Liz paused, looked down, then squeezed her eyes shut for a moment in order to hold back tears.

"That's all right! That's all right!" members of the congregation shouted.

Liz paused, attempted to regain her composure, then continued. "But God—" she said with a renewed joy and a smile on her face.

"But God!" the congregation repeated.

"But God—" Liz said again, with a sip of water this time.

"But God!" the congregation replied.

"He showed me that I had to forgive my father so that I could move on. He showed me that I had to forgive that man who left me before I was even born and receive the love from a Man who loved me even before the foundation of the world."

"Hallelujah!" a young woman from the congregation stood and shouted.

"He told me that I had to forgive this mere mortal man so that I could receive the blessings that this other Man, this great I Am Man, this King of kings and Lord of lords Man, has for me!" Liz proclaimed, and the congregation clapped.

"So I forgave him. I forgave my biological father in my heart by the time I left his house. And when I did, a sense of freedom came over me!"

The congregation clapped.

"A liberty came over me!"

Some members of the congregation stood up. Michelle and Liz stood up, as well.

"And for those of you who, like me, didn't grow up with your father or never knew your father or your father left you, I want you to know that there is a Man who will *never* leave you nor forsake you!"

Screams were heard from the congregation.

"There is a Man who will love you better than any man ever would! There is a Man who you can call on in your time of trouble. You can look to the hills from whence cometh your help. For your help!" Liz said, then added a shout. "I said *your help* comes from God!"

The entire congregation got up on their feet, and the organist took her position and starting playing shouting music.

Liz danced her way all the way back to the seat behind her on the stage next to Prophetess Parker. Liz tried to sit down but couldn't quite, so she kept dancing and shouting right at her seat, as Prophetess Parker got up and clapped her hands, as did the other speaker, Evangelist Lane.

After ten more minutes of simply praising Him, Prophetess Parker took a sip of water, wiped her forehead with a cloth napkin, then proceeded to the pulpit in order to introduce the next minister.

"Glory to God, saints, we just had *church* up in here!" Prophetess Parker said into the microphone. The congregation applauded in agreement. Prophetess Parker looked back at Liz and said, "Evangelist Coleman, we're going to have to have you back here at our church. You come with the fire!"

Liz just smiled as she regained her composure in her seat and took a sip of water.

"Well, after all that, God's still not done. We have one more speaker. Now, this young man is a minister on staff at my brother's church, Faith in Christ. He is an awesome man of God and he also told me I could share with you that he's a single, widowed father. So ladies, I know there seems to be not a lot of good men out there, but this brother is definitely a good man who is taking care of his son. He loves his little boy to life!

"So without further ado, I want to bring up here the anointed and appointed Minister Matthew Long!"

Matthew walked up to the pulpit as Prophetess Parker retreated to her seat on the stage behind the pulpit. Liz swallowed hard as he made his way to his destination. He didn't even make eye contact with her, but she was glad he didn't. She'd thought she was never going to see him again, let alone preach at the same conference. Besides, she was so sweaty from just getting her shout on she felt she wasn't prepared for him to even see her looking the way she did. At that point, she just wanted to crawl under a rock.

"Praise the Lord, everybody!" Matthew said with his signature charming smile and extremely handsome good looks. His brown three-piece pin-striped suit fit him just fine. Liz had never seen him wear that suit before.

"Well, how are y'all doing out there?" Matthew asked the congregation.

A few members said, "Fine."

"I said, how are y'all doing out there?" Matthew said, louder this time.

"Fine!" more members replied.

"Has God been good to anybody in this place?" he asked.

"Yes!" members of the congregation shouted, as some women gave a wave offering to the Lord.

"Well, all righty, then," Minister Matthew said, then gave a million-dollar smile. "Now, before I get started, I want to thank sister—excuse me, Evangelist Elizabeth Coleman— for that awesome Word we just received." Matthew turned around and clapped, and the congregation clapped right along with him.

Liz just looked at him and gave a sheepish grin, wondering why in the world he would put her on the spot like that. Was he making fun of her? Liz wished she could just exit the stage, but she couldn't in front of the whole congregation, especially since he was about to start ministering.

*Maybe I can act like I have an emergency and leave,* Liz thought. She wondered if the raised pointing finger indicating one had to leave church early worked for guest ministers, too. Probably not, she concluded and decided to just wait it out and head to the front door once the conference was over.

Matthew continued with his sermon. "To be honest, folks, I thought I had a Word from God, but it seems like God is seeming to be moving in another direction. So y'all mind if I keep flowing with the Holy Ghost?"

"Nah, go right ahead," a young woman said from the fifth row.

"The text I'm taking from for the singles today is found in Proverbs 18:22."

Minister Matthew Long read out loud from the text.

"And it reads, *Whoso findeth a wife findeth a good thing and obtaineth favor of the Lord.* I repeat, *Whoso findeth a wife findeth a good thing and obtaineth favor of the Lord.* Sounds like a Word from God to me!"

"Well," someone from the right side of the church shouted.

Minister Matthew Long continued. "Let's look at that word *favor.* Now, the word *favor* in the original Hebrew means *delight, acceptance,* and it means *good pleasure.* So we can translate this scripture to read, *Whoso findeth a wife findeth a good thing and obtaineth favor, obtaineth delight, acceptance and obtaineth good pleasure from the Lord.* Now, all these things are good, right?"

"Yes, sir!" an older man shouted from the third row.

"And all these things come when a man findeth a wife," Minister Matthew said.

Liz kept her nose buried in her Bible so as to not have any eye contact with the man preaching in the pulpit. Of all the places she would run into him again—which she actually never thought she would—she had no idea she would end up preaching at the same conference he was. Was God playing a trick on her? She already felt bad for behaving unvirtuous, which had caused her to lose him in the first place. Now she had to sit here and listen to him tell the congregation what type of woman she apparently was not. Liz squirmed in her seat. She looked up at the clock in the back of the congregation, hoping Matthew would wrap up his sermon soon.

"Elizabeth Coleman, can you come up here, please?" Matthew asked.

Liz's eyes grew big, and Michelle and Sandy just looked at each other. The congregation fell silent.

Liz stayed seated, and Prophetess Parker motioned her to go up to the pulpit.

Slowly but surely, Liz arose and made her way to the front of the stage and stood next to Matthew.

"Now, I want to apologize in advance to Prophetess Parker. But, like I said, I want to stay in the flow of the Spirit," Matthew said while holding the microphone. Prophetess Parker nodded her head for him to continue.

"Now, this here, congregation, is a woman of God," Matthew said while pointing to Liz.

Liz's knees started shaking. She knew how much he hated to be called out. *Lord, please don't let him use me as an example of the type of woman not to be. Please don't have him tell the congregation how I behaved toward him. Now is not the time for revenge, Lord, please,* Liz thought.

"A beautiful, strong, blessed woman of God," Matthew said with a smile, and some of the congregation chuckled.

"To me," Matthew said and extended his hand toward Liz, "this woman is the epitome of the Proverbs 31 woman."

Liz started to sweat bullets. She was so embarrassed. *Can I sit down now?* she thought. She'd had enough of Matthew's show-and-tell.

"To me," Matthew continued, "she is that woman the Bible talks about where it says 'her husband and children will arise and call her blessed,'" Matthew said.

"Well!" a gentleman from the sixth row shouted.

"You're blessed, Liz!" Matthew shouted suddenly.

She was flattered but also ready to take her seat. Maybe this was his way of getting back at her—by using her for his little demonstration. *I'm sure the "but" will be coming anytime now,* she thought. *Here we go.*

Liz gave a sheepish grin. She was so nervous; she felt as if she had to go to the bathroom.

"Now, to be honest, I almost—notice I said *almost*—missed God on this one," Matthew told the congregation.

*What is he talking about now?* Liz wondered.

"But I refuse to let this one go. I need to be obedient and take hold of my blessing. So Liz Coleman—" With that, Minister Matthew Long dropped down on one knee in his tailor-made suit in front of over two hundred people in the congregation.

Liz opened her mouth wide and screamed, then immediately grabbed her mouth with her hand.

Michelle and Sandy looked at each other and screamed so loudly members of the congregation looked at the two of them, then back at the stage.

Matthew grabbed Liz's left hand. "I don't have a ring yet to place on your beautiful finger, but I just feel led to do this now," Matthew said in all seriousness. "I let you get away before and I don't want to ever let you get away again. On behalf of me and on behalf of my son...where is Matt Jr.?" Matthew asked while looking out into the congregation. Mrs. Long stood up in a sharp red suit from the second row of the congregation, holding little Matt's hand.

"Bring him up here," Matthew said, and little Matt was escorted up the stage by one of the ushers. Once he reached the top step, he ran over to his dad, who grabbed him by the waist and once again faced Liz.

Matthew continued. "On behalf of me and on behalf of my son, we who love you both so dearly." Little Matt nodded his head up and down. Matthew continued, "Will you have us, Elizabeth Marie Coleman? What I'm trying to say is, will you marry me?"

Liz screamed again in utter delight and jumped up and down.

Michelle and Sandy held each other and jumped up and down as if they were on a pogo stick.

"Um, I take that as a yes?" Matthew asked and looked at his son, who nodded his head wildly in agreement.

Liz stood there shaking and nodding her head up and down wildly. "Yes!" she screamed. "Yes!"

The entire congregation jumped on their feet and gave the two of them a standing ovation. Matthew then hopped up and gave Liz a huge hug while rocking her from side to side.

Michelle and Sandy screamed for joy, as well, still jumping up and down while hugging each other.

"We're getting married! We're getting married!" Sandy proclaimed.

Liz kept holding her man tight, never wanting to ever let go.

She couldn't believe how God had taken the pain she'd felt from never knowing her father or knowing true human love from a man and turned that pain into sheer joy and happiness with a man she would soon vow to love for a lifetime.

# Chapter 39

*Always And Forever*
*Six Months Later*

The five-hundred-seat chapel at Hype for Jesus Church, adjacent to the main sanctuary, was decked out like a winter wonderland as people filled the seats in anticipation of the wedding. Even though it was only six degrees outside, a typical cold January day in Michigan, excited family members, friends, coworkers and loved ones filled the pews covered in white satin fabric in droves.

Sheer fabrics draped from the ceiling and down the walls, concealing small white Christmas lights, as a female harpist in an angelic costume played melodiously up front. The minister, clothed in a white robe, entered from the side and placed his Bible on the glass pulpit. Matthew Long, who was already up front, decked out in a white-tailed tuxedo with an ice-blue cummerbund, matching satin tie and ice-blue polished shoes, wiped his forehead, then gave dap to his best man, a fellow associate minister at his church.

A handsome usher seated Ms. Coleman, who'd dressed in a long cream two-piece suit with furry cufflinks, a skirt which draped her ankles and a matching furry hat. She sat up front and smiled at those around her, then turned around to her left and smiled at Earnestine, who was seated three rows directly behind her. Earnestine smiled and waved at Ms. Coleman in return.

Another usher simultaneously seated Matthew's parents, who entered holding hands. Mrs. Long, in her silver two-piece suit and matching box-shaped hat, smiled at her coworkers and friends seated on the left side of the sanctuary just before she and her husband, dressed in a black suit with a silver tie, had a seat.

The bridal party proudly walked down the aisle and took their places.

After a slight pause, the intro to the traditional wedding march song was played by the organist, and everyone stood on cue.

Liz walked to the center of the aisle in the back, then stood there until the song's introduction was complete. The music suddenly switched to Donnie McClurkin's "Here With You," then Liz was greeted by Mr. Backhouse, who led his only daughter down the aisle like a proud father.

Liz looked stunning in her Cinderella-like dress, complete with a hooped bottom covered in glitter and silver rhinestones and an elegant heart-shaped off-the-shoulder V-neck revealing just a hint of cleavage.

Her face was veiled and she looked like a winter princess—a winter queen as Matthew stared at her with loving adoration and glassy eyes which tell the world that he plans to be with this one for a lifetime.

Matthew wiped a single tear which had somehow escaped his right eye as Liz and her father made their way to the front. Once they made it, the minister asked, "Who gives this woman in marriage?"

Mr. Backhouse, along with Ms. Coleman, replied, "We do." Then Mr. Backhouse stepped to the side in order to allow Matthew to take his place beside his future bride.

The service continued, then the future bride and groom were asked to read their own personal vows.

Liz begins, "Matthew, words cannot explain the love I have for you right now. Your love for your son, your love for your family and, more importantly, your love for God all attracted me to you. You are a light in a dark place. You are a calm in the middle of a storm. I feel so honored that—" Liz choked up a bit "—that you would have me as your wife." She paused, looked away, then resumed staring into his eyes. "You love me in spite of myself. You loved me even when I didn't believe in love. When I didn't believe in love, you believed in me. And I just want to thank you for that." Liz wiped a tear from her eye, and her mother, from the front row, wiped a tear, as well.

Liz continued, "Matthew, I just want you to know that I will always be here for you. I will be your loving bride, from now and forever. I mean it."

Napkins were being passed all around the chapel as sniffles were heard all over the place.

Matthew wiped a tear from Liz's eye and began reciting his vows. "Liz, baby, you mean so much to me. From the first moment I saw you I knew, I knew, I *knew* that God smiled on me once again by bringing you into my life. It's been rough, but just knowing that I can't be without you one moment—one second—is enough to destroy me and enough to destroy my son." Matthew tousled the hair of little Matthew, who looked up at Liz and smiled.

"We need you in our life, Liz," Matthew said. "We love you—I love you. And I want to love you, girl, for the rest of our lives." Liz smiled wide as Matthew continued, "And I count it an honor and a privilege to have you in my life— to have you in *our* lives—forever."

The service completed, Matthew and Liz publicly received communion, then the minister proclaimed at the end of the ceremony, "By the power vested in me by the state of Michigan, I now pronounce you husband and wife! You may kiss your bride!"

Matthew and Liz kissed each other long and passionately during their very first kiss. The audience stood up and cheered, and Sandy whistled at her friend. Suddenly Matthew dipped Liz as they kept going at it. Liz's veil started to fall off, and Michelle held on to it as they continued to kiss and embrace. The photographer grabbed several shots of the seemingly never-ending kiss, as the audience kept clapping and cheering them on.

Eventually Matthew lifted Liz back up for air and the two

of them raced down the aisle of the chapel and stepped into a long white Hummer limousine, with the bridal party and parents entering the ride, as well. The two of them seemingly rode off into the sunset, with their Just Married sign especially designed by Matt Jr. on the back of the car, with ribbon and bells hanging from the sign, tied on by string.

After thirty minutes of the reception guests munching on hors d'oeuvres and listening to music until the bride and groom arrived, the bridal party, parents and bride and groom made their grand entrance in the small, intimate reception hall located in a suburb outside Detroit.

The hall decor continued with the theme of the winter wonderland. The bridal party was seated at the head table, with its white tablecloth, glass bowls filled with clear water and floating white roses in front of each table setting and centerpiece ice sculpture of an angel in prayer.

Reception guests were seated at tables of eight with chairs covered with white organza fabric and ice-blue bows tied around each one. The centerpiece on each table was a tall, slim glass vase with one single long tulip placed inside. Miniature silver bells with blue tags, which had the bride and groom's names inscribed on them along with the date, were neatly placed beside each place setting as a wedding favor.

Once dinner was served and the toasts were made, the dance floor opened and the wedding coordinator, dressed in a black dress, announced the first dance. Matthew grabbed Liz by the hand and led her onto the dance floor, splendidly decorated with artificial, white, glittery snowflakes on transparent fishing line dangling from the ceiling, a large disco ball in the center, which resembled an oversize white sparkly Christmas ornament, and a DJ booth covered in white shimmery fabric, glitter and artificial snow.

Liz and Matthew socialized to Donny Hathaway and Roberta Flack's version of "The Closer I Get to You." Liz felt as if she were in heaven as she stared deeply into Matthew's eyes, then rested her head on his broad shoulders. She let out a huge sigh. Never in her wildest dreams would she ever picture this day. She felt as if heaven were smiling on her, as if the angels were watching her in adoration. With dimmed lights and the spotlight on the two of them, it was as if no one else was in the room as Matthew held his new bride oh so close, never wanting to let go.

Once the song was over, the two of them stayed in the same position until they heard claps and cheers from their guests. They refrained from embracing for a moment, then looked at the audience, then at each other. Matthew grabbed Liz once again, then dipped her as he'd done at the wedding ceremony. Liz laughed in utter delight.

Canton Jones's song "Love Song" came on, and the dance floor filled with ballroom hustlers and couples ballroom dancing.

From her seat, Michelle looked at the dance floor, wondering if she should go out there and get her ballroom hustle on.

She had just made up her mind that she was going to go on the floor and join the other ladies when an image stood in front of her as she was bent over in her seat, making sure the strap was secured tightly on her high heel. Michelle looked up and saw David with his hand extended toward her.

"Would you care to dance?" David asked while looking extra-nice in his cream-colored suit, cream silk shirt and tan silk tie. Michelle looked up, thought about it for a moment, then went on ahead, grabbed his hand and replied, "Sure, I would love to."

David and Michelle ballroom danced, and Michelle was shocked at how smooth David's moves were on the dance floor. He kept lifting his hand, allowing Michelle to do the most favorite thing she loved to do while ballroom dancing, which is complete full turns. In the midst of his skilled moves, Michelle said, "David, I didn't know you could dance like this. You're pretty good."

David replied, "I try. Besides, we never got to go dancing before, so my dancing skills are yet another thing you have yet to learn about me. You learn something new about me every day, huh?"

Michelle looked deep into his eyes as she continued to dance and said, "You're right. I do learn something new every day." After a pause Michelle added, "David, I'm sorry."

David kept spinning Michelle around and said, "Don't apologize, just dance. Let's maximize the moment right now. Let's never let this moment slip away from our memory bank."

Michelle looked at him with a smirky grin.

While dancing, David added, "Michelle, I head back to Atlanta on Monday."

Michelle did not say a word in response. What was there to say?

David continued, "You know, being at this wedding and all helped me realize what's really important."

Michelle gave him a suspicious glance as the two of them continued to dance.

David added, "Michelle, you're very special to me, whether you choose to believe it or not. And Matthew's vows to Liz today taught me about the importance of not letting an opportunity pass by."

Michelle kept dancing, when suddenly David, in the middle of the dance floor, dropped down to one knee.

Everyone looked at the two of them, including Sandy, who was seated at the table, munching on what was left of the wedding cake.

David, on his knee, grabbed Michelle's right hand and asked, "Michelle, I really care about you, and if you're willing, I want to give our relationship another chance."

Michelle looked around, partly excited, partly embarrassed. *Was he going to pop the question in front of all these strangers, at Liz and Matthew's wedding reception?* she thought. She wasn't sure if that would be flattering or rude.

David took a deep breath, then asked, "Michelle, will you be my girlfriend again?"

Michelle just looked down at David and smiled as if he was the most adorable person in the world.

When he didn't receive an immediate response, he continued, "I know, with my being in Atlanta and all, it'll be like a long-distance relationship, but I know with God all things are—"

Michelle placed her index finger on top of his lips and said, "Shhh. Let's just maximize the moment, okay? Now shut up and dance, David Parker."

With that, David got up, taking that as a yes, then held Michelle tight and she squeezed him back.

"Sure, baby," she said in his ear, "I'll be your girlfriend again." David hugged Michelle even tighter and rocked her as tears filled Michelle's eyes. *Thank God for second chances,* she thought. *Praise the Lord.*

Onlookers cheered on David and Michelle, while Sandy, from the table up front, flashed a fake smile toward the two of them while secretly thinking about her own life and lack of a man—or even lack of an escort to the wedding.

Sandy grabbed a wineglass filled with sparkling apple cider and took a big swig, then wiped the side of her mouth with a napkin. She was caught off guard by a fine figure who looked to be about six-four in a black tux, extending his hand toward her and then saying in a deep, husky voice, "Excuse me, my name is Dexter. Dexter Washington. I couldn't help but notice you from across the room and, I must say, you're very beautiful."

Sandy stared at the man in shock and almost felt as if she had to regain her composure because of how fine he was.

"Sandy," she said in a normal tone, not wanting to show signs of her internal excitement. "Sandra A. Moore," she said while shaking his hand.

"Mind if I sit down?" he asked.

"Sure, go right ahead," Sandy said, then motioned him to sit in the empty seat beside her.

Dexter sat down, then pulled his seat close to her and said, "I'm sure you hear this all the time, but I am dead serious. Sandy—or Sandra—you are drop-dead gorgeous."

"Thanks," Sandy said with a sheepish grin, "and you can call me Sandy."

"Well, um, okay, Sandy," Dexter continued. "To be honest, when I saw you come down the aisle during the wedding ceremony, I thought to myself, *Dexter Washington, now, that's a fine woman.*"

"Thank you," Sandy said while blushing. "You're too kind."

"I don't mean to be forward, but, uh, are you seeing someone?"

"No," Sandy replied quickly.

"Well, um, do you mind if we exchange numbers? Maybe we can go out sometime. I'd love to take you out in my Mercedes-Benz, parked out front."

*Did he say Mercedes-Benz?* Sandy thought. *Calm down, Sandy, calm down. Don't let the exterior excite you. Slow your roll. But, my goodness, Lord. Can a sister just have a little fun?*

"Um, I'm not sure…maybe. Are you saved, Mr. Washington?" Sandy asked, then held her breath.

Dexter popped his collar and said, "Why, yes, I am saved. I'm actually flattered you asked me that question. You see, I happen to be looking for a nice, good, *saved* woman myself."

*Thank you, Jesus!* Sandy thought. However, before she did

the Holy Ghost shout on the inside, she wanted to be sure of one more thing.

"Well, praise God, that's nice," she said calmly. "It's nice that you're saved and all. However, I do have another question for you."

"What's that?" Dexter asked with gleaming eyes and curled lips.

Sandy then asked, "You're saved...but are you for real?"

Because even the smartest women can make
relationship mistakes…

ACCLAIMED AUTHOR

# JEWEL DIAMOND TAYLOR

*You*
DESERVE
MORE

A straight-to-the point book that will empower women
and help them overcome such self-defeating emotions as
insecurity, desperation, jealousy, loneliness…all factors that
can keep you in a destructive cycle of unloving, unfulfilling
relationships. Through the powerful insights and life-lessons
in this book, you will learn to build a relationship that's
strong enough to last a lifetime.

"Jewel Diamond Taylor captivates audiences. She moves the spirit."
—Susan L. Taylor, Editorial Director, *Essence* magazine

*Available the first week of January, wherever books are sold.*

**www.kimanipress.com**

KPJDT1550108TR

A volume of heartwarming devotionals
that will nourish your soul...

# NORMA DeSHIELDS BROWN

*Joy*

COMES THIS MORNING

Norma DeShields Brown's life suddenly changed
when her only son was tragically taken from her
by a senseless act. Consumed by grief, she began
an intimate journey that became
*Joy Comes This Morning.*

Filled with thoughtful devotions, Scripture readings
and words of encouragement, this powerful book
will guide you on a spiritual journey that will sustain
you throughout the years.

*Available the first week of November
wherever books are sold.*

**www.kimanipress.com**

GET THE GENUINE LOVE
YOU DESERVE...

NATIONAL BESTSELLING AUTHOR

# Vikki Johnson

## Addicted to COUNTERFEIT LOVE

Many people in today's world are unable to recognize
what a genuine loving partnership should be and
often sabotage one when it does come along. In this
moving volume, Vikki Johnson offers memorable
words that will help readers identify destructive love
patterns and encourage them to demand the love
that they are entitled to.

*Available the first week of October wherever books are sold.*

NEW SPIRIT
™

**www.kimanipress.com**

KPVJ0381007TR

*Forgiveness takes courage...*

# A MEASURE OF
# *Faith*

## MAXINE BILLINGS

With her loving husband, a beautiful home and two wonderful children, Lynnette Montgomery feels very blessed. But a sudden car accident starts a chain of events that tests her faith, and pulls to the forefront memories of a very painful childhood. At forty years of age, Lynnette comes to see that it takes a measure of faith to help one through the pains of life.

**"An enlightening read with an endearing family theme."**
**—*Romantic Times BOOKreviews***
**on *The Breaking Point***

***Available the first week of July***
***wherever books are sold.***

A soul-stirring, compelling
journey of self-discovery…

# journey
## into My Brother's Soul

*Maria D. Dowd*

Bestselling author of
*Journey to Empowerment*

A memorable collection of essays, prose and poetry,
reflecting the varied experiences that men of color face
throughout life. Touching on every facet of living—love,
marriage, fatherhood, family—these candid personal
contributions explore the essence of what it means to
be a man today.

**"*Journey to Empowerment* will lead you on a
healing journey and will lead to a great love of self,
and a deeper understanding of the many roles we
all must play in life."—*Rawsistaz Reviewers***

Coming the first week of May
wherever books are sold.